BE A
MASTERPEACE
NOT A
MONSTERPIECE

Walk the Path of Peace,
Purpose, and Power

WHO ARE YOU - BOOK 1

MARIA OLON-TSAROUCHA

For permission requests, write to the publisher addressed "Attention: Book Rights and Permission," at the address below.
Published in the United States of America

ISBN 9798992687774

Supraconscious You
150 Bogert St, Totowa, NJ 07512
info@supraconscious.co

Order Information and Rights Permission:
Quantity sales. Special discounts might be available on quantity purchases by corporations, associations, and others. For details, contact the publisher at the address above. For Book Rights Adaptation and other Rights Permission. Send us an email at info@supraconscious.co

Supraconscious You
https://supraconscious.co/

To Konstantinos and Elia,
whose presence paints light into my every breath— and to the
brave hearts who hold this book in their hands, ready to meet
themselves beneath the noise of the world.

This is for you—
the seekers, the feelers, the unbecoming and becoming, the ones
who walk through shadow with eyes full of wonder.

May these words be a compass to the truth you've always
carried:

We are not broken. We are becoming whole.

We are not lost.

We are art in motion.

You are—
a masterpiece

Contents

This book is rooted in the research, study, theory, and methodology originally introduced in *SUPRACONSCIOUS: The Genius Within You*. It translates that profound body of work into a living, breathing journey—accessible, grounded, and meant for everyday awakening.

Each chapter, roadmap, exercise, visualization, and reflective question holds the rhythm of your soul's evolution. This is not abstract philosophy—it's an invitation to rise beyond inherited patterns, dissolve illusions, and create a life that reflects the extraordinary truth of who you are

The Architecture of a Supraconscious Life

Chapter 2: The Blueprint of Your Mind 27

Chapter 4: Embracing Your Story   62

Chapter 5: Aligning with Your Purpose   73

Chapter 6: Ruling The Inner Kingdom 85

Chapter 9: Fear of Death, Fear of Life 125

Chapter X: Where Do You Hold Your Power?   144

Chapter 11: The Ultimate Quest for Dynamic Living 175

Chapter 13: The Fulfillment of Deepest Desires   209

Chapter 14: Drafting Your Masterpiece Life   226

Chapter 15: Masterpiece or Monsterpiece 236

My Masterpeace: The ReBirth 242

Always Know

LIFE HAPPENS AS YOU

My Calling

My dear fellow traveler—perhaps you are seeking meaning. Perhaps you carry questions too tender to name. Whatever brought you here, know this:

You are a masterpiece among masterpieces.

Not because of perfection, but because your very existence is an intentional work of art. A masterpiece does not mean flawless; it means singular, irreplaceable, and alive with purpose.

You are a singular note in the great symphony of existence, a brushstroke on the vast canvas of life.

Do you know how exquisite you are?
How powerful?
How divinely designed!

It is no coincidence that you are reading these words right now.

It is no coincidence that you are here in this moment, standing exactly where you are, feeling precisely what you feel.

It is no coincidence that life has unfolded as it has—this day, this month, this year—bringing you to this very place at this precise moment.

Let me be clear: this chapter is not only about wonder, nor only about destiny, nor only about personal transformation. It is about one essential invitation—the call to awaken to yourself. The words you are reading are here to remind you that beneath the noise of your daily life, there is a deeper truth waiting. You are not merely passing through existence; you are meant to participate in it consciously. My purpose in these opening pages is simple: to help you remember that your life is not an accident and that within you rests the power to live as the masterpiece you already are.

Everything in your life—the struggles, the victories, the whispers of intuition, the unexpected turns—has led you here. There is a greater reason you find yourself in this moment, holding these thoughts, these questions, this longing for something more. Perhaps you feel it as a quiet pull within, a knowing beyond logic, an invitation to step into a deeper understanding of who you are.

The universe is not random. Every encounter, every challenge, and every moment of stillness or movement is a thread in the vast tapestry of your becoming. There is a reason you are here. A reason you are seeking. A reason you are awakening.

But even if you think none of this is true.

Even if you believe that life is pure chance, that there is no hidden meaning, no greater unfolding.

Even if you tell yourself that you don't believe in deeper truths or in the possibility of something more.

You are still here.
You are still holding this book.
You are still reading these lines.

So, tell me—why is that?

Something in you brought you to this moment. Maybe curiosity. Maybe resistance. Perhaps it is a longing you don't fully understand yet. But whatever it is, it exists. It is real.

So, what if—just for now—you allowed yourself to wonder?

I welcome you.

I am honored that you are reading these lines, thoughts, and truths I am eager to share. But before we embark on this journey together, allow me to share my journey, a tapestry woven with threads of art, research, and a deep quest for understanding human nature and consciousness.

My name is Maria.

I am an artist, a researcher, an educator, and an author— driven by an unquenchable thirst for knowledge and a deep love for the mysteries of existence. More importantly, I am a servant of life's wonders, eternally in pursuit of awakening. Not a sudden event, but the steady unfolding of awareness when one begins to see life with new eyes.

For the last eighteen years, my path has been one of exploring philosophical systems that illuminate personal growth and consciousness. But that journey did not begin in peace—it began with disruption. My awakening started when I realized I was inhabiting a life not of my design, but one shaped by the expectations of family and society. Though I had achieved success as an actor and director, the roles I played felt like masks in a narrative that was never truly mine. I remember standing in full costume backstage during a performance, the applause still echoing, and feeling hollow. I smiled and bowed, yet inside I heard, 'Whose story are you living?'

One quiet night, this illusion cracked. An inner voice broke through the noise and asked a question too urgent to ignore:

"Who are you?"

That question propelled me into a profound transformation, from unconscious existence into the search for a higher awareness—what I would later recognize as the Supraconscious state: the deeper current of being that lies beyond ordinary thought yet within every one of us.

The years that followed were not easy. As a single mother facing financial instability, I questioned everything—my purpose, my needs, my desires. These questions became the anchors of my conscious journey. Immersed in theater, I felt a deeper pull, a whisper urging me to look inward. This calling led me to meditation, Eastern philosophies, neuroscience, and eventually the startling revelations of quantum physics.

In this process, I began to see myself as more than an actor upon life's stage. I became a vessel for something greater. This shift sustained me even in my darkest hours, such as when I feared losing my son to addiction. His eventual recovery became living proof of the transformative power of aligning one's path with a higher truth.

With determination, my children, and only a few possessions, I carried this realization across an ocean, beginning anew in America. That leap was more than a relocation—it was a declaration that I would live consciously, no longer shaped by the world's expectations, but guided by the deeper wisdom within.

The essence of this journey is simple: life, when not consciously directed, can feel uncontrollable. Yet within us, the Supraconscious offers freedom from inherited scripts and societal imprints. My story stands as witness that awakening is possible for anyone. When you turn inward and ask who you are beneath the noise, you begin to unleash the masterpiece that has always lived inside you.

By definition, humans are actors responding to every small, significant, or seemingly insignificant decision we make.

Our fleeting thoughts, buried emotions, and unconscious habits shape our personal stories and the very fabric of history. What we do now will become the past of our progeny.

But what if we were more than just actors? What if we were creators of our lives? What if the stage of life wasn't something we simply moved across but something we could consciously shape?

For most of my life, I played my roles diligently. I worked tirelessly to be a good daughter so my parents would be proud and to be a good wife and mother so my family would be happy. I devoted myself to my art, determined to express something authentic and worthy. I played every role with devotion—a friend, a provider, a woman standing strong in a world that constantly asked for more. And yet, life felt like an endless game of invisible losses, a long-term gamble where I sacrificed pieces of myself for dreams that dissolved like mist.

And then, in a single moment, in a shift of mind, I understood.

There was a moment when this truth revealed itself to me—one of those rare instances when time collapses, and an idea is too powerful to let go. I was asleep when it struck. A force, a calling, an inspiration pulled me awake. I sat up in the darkness, desperately grasping for pen and paper, trying to capture the thought before it slipped into the vast unconscious reservoir of forgotten dreams.

It wasn't in success, applause, validation, or security that I found myself. I found myself in surrender, in embracing the losses as much as the gifts, in standing still long enough to hear the whisper of my soul, in loving who I am, not for what I have achieved but for the simple, sacred fact that I exist, I am here now, I am alive.

I had spent years lost in the struggle of understanding— trying to make sense of complex equations in chemistry and physics. Mathematics seemed like a language I was not meant to speak. And yet, I was obsessed with what lay beyond numbers: the invisible forces that shape our choices, emotions, and destinies. I discovered something that changed my entire life. It wasn't an external lesson; it was a memory—something already within me, waiting to be recognized.

I may not speak in numbers or financial formulas, but I understand the language of silence, of color, of connection. My intelligence is woven through story, through stillness, through wonder—and it is no less profound.

I know art, I know books, and I am a great communicator. I love nature and the animal kingdom. I feel the earth's rhythms, the wisdom in silence, the poetry hidden between moments. And I finally understand that science is not separate from art, philosophy from physics, or emotion from reason. They are all one—aligned, woven together in a cosmic dance, giving us answers only if we allow ourselves to reach beyond ordinary thought.

In that deep realization, I found something more profound than knowledge—I found peace.

Because I found peace not in answers but in deeper questions, I now write not to teach, but to travel beside you—as someone who's been lost and found, and still walks.

This book is not a lesson. It is an invitation.

An invitation to step beyond knowledge and into wisdom. To dive into the divine questioning that has lived inside you since the beginning.

To surrender—to the beauty of becoming who you were always meant to be.

We live in a world that often separates us from our true nature. Yet beneath the noise and beyond fear, your inner genius waits—ready to be ignited. This journey is about transcending the limitations you are not meant to carry and rising into the fullness of who you are.

My calling—the unique way my masterpiece comes alive— is to help you remember your own. A calling is not merely a career or role; it is the resonance of your soul living in alignment with truth.

I wish to guide you in aligning your life with your highest self—where clarity replaces confusion, freedom dissolves fear, and your days reflect the masterpiece you were born to create.

It is not about becoming someone new; it's about returning to the truth of who you've always been.

Throughout this book, I will frequently use four words: masterpiece, awakening, calling, and Supraconscious. Each is a thread in the same tapestry. To awaken is to hear your calling. To live your calling is to reveal the masterpiece within you. The Supraconscious is the hidden current that carries you there, if you choose to listen. These words will recur not as lofty ideals, but as landmarks to guide you on your journey.

Let's begin with courage, love, and unwavering faith in your divine unfolding.

Settle in. Breathe deep.

The story is yours now.

CHAPTER 1
The Awakening

The Gentle (or Not-So-Gentle) Slap from the Universe

With love—and just a little tough love—I must tell you:

Awakening isn't always wrapped in candlelight and bliss; sometimes, it's a rude awakening, like a cosmic cold splash to the face. Uncomfortable, yes. But essential.

Sometimes, it feels like someone poured cold water on your face before you even had your morning coffee. Not fun, but necessary.

And here's the real kicker: You hold the power to wake up or wait for life to do it. It is not a passive process but an active choice for your growth and self-awareness.

Alert: Life rarely whispers; it roars when you've waited too long to listen. It prefers the emotional equivalent of a marching band in your living room.

I didn't choose my awakening; it came barreling in like a surprise guest who forgot to knock—and stayed. One day, I looked around at the life I had built and thought, "Wait a minute... whose dream am I living? Because this one doesn't fit." I remember standing in my kitchen at 3 a.m., holding a cup of tea, staring into nothing—feeling like a stranger in my own life.

I had done what many of us do: I followed the dotted lines on a life map I didn't draw—smiled when I wanted to cry—played the role. Memorized the script. Somewhere in all that acting, I lost the author—the real me.

If this sounds even a little familiar, you're not alone. So many of us live by default rather than by design. We follow shoulds instead of soul. We go to school for the job, not the joy. We marry for timing, not truth. That's a 'should.' A 'soul' path whispers in quieter tones—purpose, alignment, curiosity. This shared experience binds us in our journey toward personal growth and self-awareness.

But then something flickers—maybe during a sleepless night, a breakup, a failure that shakes you, or even something as small as a question whispered inside: *Is this it?*

That flicker is the beginning. It's the soul saying,

"There's more. Come find it."

That is the awakening.

It's not about becoming someone else; it's about returning to the person you were before the world told you who to be. The quiet voice before the noise. The wild light before the masks.

It felt like discovering a hidden door in a room I thought I'd already explored. I hadn't noticed it before—but now, I could never unsee it.

The tragedy isn't that we get shaken awake; the tragedy is when we ignore it—push the call to the side, hit snooze, and hope life gets easier without us having to change.

That's why the first chapter begins with the awakening. Because starting consciously, with courage and even a bit of clumsiness, is a thousand times better than being caught unprepared. Searching for who you are *after* the storm is more brutal. I know—because I searched, stumbled, and scraped my knees on every truth I found.

But I also discovered something miraculous: the Golden Triangle.

It's my foundation, compass, and secret for rising out of confusion and into clarity.

Welcome to your awakening.

The Golden Triangle: Mapping Your Mind

Imagine your mind as a triangle—three powerful forces holding equal corners, each pulling in its direction. It's like an intense game of mental tug-of-war. And guess who's in the middle, being stretched, squeezed, and spun around? That's right: *You.*

But here's the thing—this isn't a battle; it's a relationship. When you understand the dynamics, you stop being the rope and start becoming the one who calls the shots.

Let me introduce your mental dream team:

The Ego – The Overprotective Bodyguard

The Ego is the mind's security guard—built from fear, rooted in control. It believes safety is sameness and thrives on predictability. Thinks it's the main character, loves control, and panics over embarrassing moments from ten years ago. Your Ego craves safety and predictability. It follows the rules, avoids risks, and seeks validation. It's like a strict but well-intentioned life coach, always whispering:

- *Stay in your comfort zone—it's safer here.*
- *Don't take that leap. What if you fail?*
- *Follow the rules. Be what people expect you to be.*

The Ego isn't your enemy; it's simply doing its job—keeping you alive and protected. It learned early on that avoiding danger equals survival. But what it doesn't understand is that growth requires stepping into the unknown.

Think of it as a well-meaning but outdated operating system. It was programmed in childhood, based on past experiences, but it struggles to adapt to the evolving, expansive being you are becoming.

Take a moment to journal: What is your ego most afraid of? Rejection? Exposure? Not being in control? Whose voice is echoing here?

Here's the truth: Most of our deepest fears are inherited, not chosen. But the beauty is—you don't have to carry them anymore.

You get to decide what stays and what dissolves. You get to rewrite the script.

So thank your ego for trying to protect you. Then tell it gently: *"I'm safe now. I choose differently."*

That's where the separation from your ego begins—when you stop identifying with it and start observing.

The Subconscious: The Secret Keeper

Think of your subconscious as the basement of your mind. It's filled with memories, emotions, and old beliefs you didn't even realize existed. The subconscious stirs with untapped potential beneath the surface of your everyday awareness. It whispers secrets you've buried and hints at paths not yet taken.

Remember when you were a child, brimming with creativity and curiosity? That part of you is still alive, waiting to reconnect. Often dismissed as fleeting reactions, your emotions hold the key to unlocking this deeper self. Like an actor delving into a role, you can tap into the emotional memories of your past—not to dwell in nostalgia but to rediscover the vibrant authenticity that once defined you. By reconnecting with the child within, you journey back to your true self, where wonder and wisdom exist.

Somewhere along the way, society started teaching you rules: Be responsible, be realistic, and stop dreaming. Little by little, you locked your natural creativity and wisdom away in that basement.

Here's the thing: just because those beliefs have been in storage doesn't mean they can't be dusted off, questioned, and rewritten.

That's what awakening is all about—reclaiming the parts of yourself you forgot.

Your subconscious is a deep archive—layered with memories, fears, and stories, both true and inherited. It holds onto:

- *The words you heard growing up ("Money is hard to earn." "You must work tirelessly to be worthy.")*
- *The emotional imprints of past failures, rejections, and heartbreaks*
- *The unconscious patterns you repeat without realizing*

The subconscious doesn't distinguish between truth and falsehood; it simply records. If you were told as a child, *"You're not good at math,"* your subconscious stores it as fact, quietly shaping your reality for years.

Many of the obstacles in your life are **not real**—they are subconscious programs running in the background, dictating your thoughts and actions.

But here's the good news:

You can rewrite the script.

Take a moment to listen—not with your mind but your heart.

What beliefs have quietly shaped your life, like invisible hands guiding your choices?

Maybe it's the idea that love must be earned, or that vulnerability equals weakness, or that productivity defines your worth. That success requires suffering, and one's worth depends on how much one does, gives, or proves. These patterns often run so deep that we mistake them for truth.

Ask yourself:

- *Do these beliefs still honor who I am becoming?*
- *Are they outdated stories, rooted in fear, passed down from generations that didn't know any better?*

Here's the miracle: You have the power to choose again. Thank the old patterns for how they once tried to protect you—and lovingly release them.

You are no longer here to survive the past; you are here to live your truth and shape your life not from fear but from love. That's where liberation begins.

The Higher Self – The Calm Inner Sage

While your subconscious holds onto old fears, your higher self acts like a cosmic GPS, nudging you toward your highest potential. It communicates through intuition, moments of inspiration, and gut feelings that tell you, *"This is right for me."*

Most of us ignore these signs because they don't always make logical sense. But logic is only one piece of the puzzle. Your higher self doesn't concern itself with small details like *"Will this decision make everyone happy?"* It deals with truth. When you begin to listen, life shifts in ways you never imagined.

Though the world around you may seem chaotic, a hidden order exists beneath the noise—a pattern woven by your higher self. This part of you whispers encouragement when you stand on the edge of fear, nudging you toward your highest potential. It is more than a spiritual presence; it is the essence of your creativity and the architect of your higher path. There's no need to fear terms like *"higher self."* These are not abstract, mystical concepts meant to separate you from reality; they are reminders of your potential and your essence beyond fear, doubt, and limitation. Your *higher self* is not external or unreachable; it is the deepest, most authentic part of who you are.

This understanding is your greatest gift: *free will*. You are free to observe yourself—not with judgment, guilt, or shame, but with love, empathy, and curiosity. True self-awareness is not about labeling yourself as "good" or "bad" but recognizing the patterns, beliefs, and emotions that shape your life. It is the ability to step back, see yourself clearly, and gently choose a path that aligns with peace, growth, and truth.

When you observe yourself with love instead of fear, transformation occurs effortlessly. There is no need to force change or suppress emotions—only the need to *see* with an open heart. Through this awareness, you align with your true nature, where wisdom, joy, and purpose flow naturally.

Awakening is not about rejecting responsibility or denying reality; it's about realizing you have a say in how your reality unfolds. You are the creator of your own experience. The moment you step back and observe yourself with curiosity rather than judgment, you unlock a new level of freedom.

The signs are subtle yet persistent—the sudden pull of inspiration, the quiet knowing that defies logic, the deep resonance you feel when something aligns with your true purpose. These are not coincidences; they are guideposts on your journey to awakening.

When the higher self whispers, you must listen:

- *You are more powerful than you realize.*

- *Your dreams exist for a reason—because they matter to you.*
- *As you strive forward, never forget this truth: nothing is missing from you. Wholeness is already your birthright.*

But for many of us, the Ego and Subconscious run the show while the Higher Self waits in the background, saying, "Hey! I am always here. I have great ideas!"

Awakening is about shifting this balance—moving away from autopilot and allowing your higher self to take the lead. The more you quiet the noise of the ego and redesign the patterns of the subconscious, the more precise your connection with your higher self becomes.

Journal Prompt: Sit in stillness for five minutes. Ask your Higher Self, 'What truth do you want me to know right now?' Let the words emerge.

The challenge is identifying who's calling the shots and nudging the balance toward awakening. The ego will keep you stuck; the subconscious may replay that awkward handshake, while the higher self holds the wisdom that could blow your mind if you just tune in.

The Power of Alignment: Restoring the Golden Triangle Within

The Golden Triangle: A Quick Guide

The Golden Triangle represents the harmony of your inner world—three voices that shape your choices, fears, and freedom. Understanding them provides the map to alignment.

- **Ego** – The protector. It seeks safety, approval, and survival, often clinging to the past or fearing the future. When balanced, it offers structure and groundedness.

- **Subconscious** – The keeper of memories. It stores your patterns, beliefs, and hidden scripts—both empowering and limiting. When awakened, it becomes a reservoir of creativity and intuition.

- **Higher Self** – The calm inner sage. It whispers wisdom, guiding you toward growth, peace, and purpose. It is not outside you; it is the most authentic part of you.

- **The Golden Triangle** – The interplay of these three. When Ego, Subconscious, and Higher Self work in unity, you step into alignment—living not as fragments but as a masterpiece unfolding from within.

Now that you understand these three forces, how can you **shift the power dynamic?**

- *Listen actively to your Ego without letting it dictate your choices.*

When fear arises, acknowledge it: *"I hear you, but I choose a different path."*

- *Engage with your Subconscious and renovate outdated patterns.*
- *Identify beliefs that no longer serve you and replace them with empowering truths.*
- *Tune into your Higher Self and act on its wisdom.*

Make space for intuition, creativity, and moments of stillness where profound knowing can emerge.

You are not confined to old lines on a page. You are free to choreograph a new dance, one that reflects the truth of who you are.

The question is:

Who do you choose to become?

The Present Moment: A Portal to Alignment

The present moment is not just a fleeting second in time; it is the only place where real life unfolds and genuine transformation begins. When you return to this moment repeatedly, you start to experience life as a direct, felt reality rather than a concept.

Henri Cartier-Bresson, the visionary photographer, once spoke of *the decisive moment*—that precise point when everything aligns in perfect harmony. The same is true within you.

The Golden Triangle—your Ego, Subconscious, and Higher Self—finds its best balance and clarity when anchored in the now.

- *The ego relaxes, no longer trapped in past regrets or future anxieties.*
- *The subconscious becomes accessible, its patterns gently revealed through awareness.*
- *The higher self speaks, not in noise, but in stillness— through intuition, peace, and presence.*

To train your awareness of the present is to reclaim your power. Each moment offers a sacred chance to observe, choose, and realign. Savor it, witness it, and let it guide you back to yourself.

Eckhart Tolle refers to this as *The Power of Now*—not a concept to understand, but a space to live from.

In truth, there is no past to repair and no future to chase.

There is only *this*.

And in *this*, everything becomes possible.

This moment.

Awakening to Presence: The Beginning of Eckhart's Truth

Eckhart Tolle, spiritual teacher and author of *The Power of Now*, experienced a radical shift into awareness after years of inner turmoil. His journey exemplifies how an ordinary person can awaken to enlightenment and find their true path in life. He was not born a spiritual master; he was an everyday person plagued by anxiety, depression, and deep suffering. His transformation occurred at the peak of his despair when he questioned, *Who is the 'I' that cannot live with myself?* This realization shattered his identification with the ego, leading him to profound peace and presence.

His story teaches that enlightenment is not reserved for mystics or monks; it is accessible to anyone willing to step out of their thoughts and embrace the present moment. Tolle shows that suffering often acts as a catalyst for awakening, and by letting go of mental identification with the past and future, one can discover true purpose, inner peace, and fulfillment. His experience proves that enlightenment is not about external success but about shifting consciousness and living fully in the *now*.

Shining Now: Living the Golden Triangle Moment by Moment

A Simple Process to Align in the Present Moment

Every moment, you are offered a choice: to live from reaction or awareness. The Golden Triangle is not a destination; it's a way of being. Below is a five-step process to help you experience this alignment right here, right now:

Recognize

Take a deep breath and gently observe the story you're living. Whose voice is shaping your decisions?

Is this your soul's path—or the echo of someone else's fear or expectation?

Illuminate

Picture the Golden Triangle: Ego, Subconscious, and Higher Self. Which part is leading in this moment?

Where is there tension? Where is there truth?

Let this inner map help you recompose the story you are living.

Embrace

Turn toward your Higher Self—the quiet, loving presence within.

Feel its acceptance. Let go of the need to be perfect, understood, or validated. In this stillness, feel held. You are already enough.

Reflect

Close your eyes and remember a moment from childhood when you felt pure joy, freedom, or curiosity.

That spark still lives within you. Let it guide you.

Reconnecting with this innocence revives your divine creativity and awakens profound truth.

Awaken

In this space of clarity, ask: What would love choose now? Let your awareness illuminate what is real.

By choosing presence, you transform your reality—gently, radically, and beautifully.

The Power of Inner Alignment

In this moment, you are not a fragment.
You are not your past.
You are a living harmony, a soul designed to live in truth, with all three aspects of yourself working together in unity.

Alignment recognizes your wholeness. You are not a project to be completed or a puzzle missing pieces. You are already whole, and from this wholeness, your Higher Self speaks. The more you allow your Ego, Subconscious, and Higher Self to collaborate in harmony, the more you experience this truth—not as a concept, but as a lived reality.

As you explore the question, *"Who am I?"* know that this inquiry is the cornerstone of your transformation. It ignites a process that moves you from living unconsciously to embracing the vibrant truth of your Awareness. The moment you begin to question, you have already started to awaken.

Unity is the art of living. Unity is how the masterpiece unfolds—from the inside out. You are not becoming whole; you already are.

This wholeness is not the destination—it is the doorway. Recognizing your unity means standing at the threshold of a new way of living, where awareness guides your choices and love directs your steps. The question "Who am I?" is not just reflection; it is initiation. The moment you dare to ask, you are already on the path of awakening.

Now, the journey deepens. In the next chapter, we will step inside the architecture of your mind—exploring the Ego, Subconscious, and Supraconscious in greater depth. These hidden landscapes shape your choices, fears, and freedom. By mapping this inner terrain, you will begin to see clearly how alignment unfolds in daily life—and how your Higher Self has been guiding you all along.

Having taken the first step toward awakening, the next chapter delves into understanding the intricate layers of your mind. Unlock the secrets of your unconscious, conscious, and supraconscious levels, and learn how each influences your journey.

Ready to map your mental terrain?

Let's continue.

CHAPTER 2
The Blueprint of Your Mind

Your Brain: The Odd Couple Running Your Life

If your brain were a sitcom, the left and right hemispheres would be the ultimate odd couple—one's a methodical planner, the other a wild dreamer. Together, they script every scene of your life.

Let's break it down:

The Brilliant Logic of the Left Hemisphere: Meet Your Inner Accountant

The brain's left hemisphere loves logic, rules, numbers, lists, and structure. It's the part of you that double-checks the restaurant bill and organizes your sock drawer by color. It also houses anxiety, fear, control issues, and your ego. So if you've ever overanalyzed a text message or questioned your worth after one awkward meeting, blame this guy.

Right Hemisphere Playground: Where Wonder Lives

This hemisphere is a playground of intuition, imagination, and gut feelings. It paints vivid daydreams, helps you sense things before they happen, and urges you to take that spontaneous road trip. It's where faith, creativity, and spontaneity thrive. If you've ever had a 'feeling' about something that turned out to be right, your right brain gives you a smug high-five. It's a source of inspiration and motivation, guiding you toward your true path.

Science loves the left brain; art adores the right. But the real magic happens when they work together.

What Moved the Hand of Da Vinci?

Leonardo da Vinci exemplifies the perfect balance between the right and left brain. As a polymath, he fused artistic creativity (*The Mona Lisa*) with scientific analysis (anatomy, engineering). His right brain fueled his imagination and intuition, while his left brain applied logic and precision. By integrating both hemispheres, he saw no divide between art and science, using one to enhance the other.

The problem?

Most people overuse the left brain, micromanaging their lives while ignoring the right brain's intuitive whispers. But here's the kicker—your right brain is the side that never lies. It's the part of you that senses truth before your rational mind catches up.

And like Da Vinci, you too can unlock creative genius—not by choosing sides, but by letting reason and wonder dance.

As the saying goes, *"The mind asks the questions, but the heart gives the answers."*

Left Brain vs. Right Brain vs. Balance

We often lean too far to one side of the brain—or swing wildly between both. Let's meet three characters who illustrate this.

- **George (Left Brain All the Way)**
George lives by the spreadsheet. He plans his day down to the minute and color-codes his grocery list. He's organized, reliable, and precise—but when life throws a curveball, he panics because it wasn't on the schedule.

- **Sophia (Right Brain Dreamer)**
Sophia is a whirlwind of creativity. She'll start five paintings before breakfast, forget to eat lunch, and write poetry on napkins at dinner. Inspiring, yes—but bills, deadlines, and dentist appointments often slip through the cracks.

- **Alex (The Balancer)**
  Alex blends structure with spontaneity. They can brainstorm wild ideas in the morning and turn them into a practical action plan by night. Alex isn't perfect, but they move forward with both clarity and flow.

Takeaway: Balance is key.

You need logic, but you also need intuition. You need plans, but you also need flow.

Language: More Than Just Words

Our words don't just describe what the brain thinks—they help shape what it believes to be true.

Ancient Greek wisdom tells us: "*The catharsis of pain brings about healing.*"

That means when you express something sincerely, you release its weight. But language is tricky—it's more than just words; **it's a code of reality**, shaping how you perceive the world.

Every conversation is a **constructed reality** molded by personal experiences, culture, and internal maps you may not realize you are using. For example, take the Greek word "anthropos" (human). According to Socrates, humans are the only creatures who observe, reflect, and comment on what they see. But isn't the word itself just a construction? What if we had called humans "clouds" or "tigers"? Would that change how we see ourselves?

Consider Yorgos Lanthimos's film *Dogtooth*, where a family creates bizarre language, redefining everyday words. In *Dogtooth*, words like 'sea' are redefined to mean 'armchair,' showing how language can entirely warp one's sense of what is real.

It reminds us that words don't just describe reality; they create it.

Here's something we rarely pause to consider:

The language you use isn't just a way to describe your world— it's how you design it.

Every sentence, whether whispered in your mind or spoken aloud, is a signal. Every word is a choice. And your brain? It's always listening. Not just passively—it takes your words as truth, even in sarcasm, frustration, or habit.

And that's where the problem begins.

Most of us speak with **zero awareness** of how powerful our words are.

Think about the things you say to yourself without even blinking:

"I can't handle this."
"I always screw things up at the worst time."
"No matter what I do, it's never enough."
"I don't deserve more."

Sometimes, we say these things silently. Other times, we vocalize them, not just to ourselves but to those around us:

"You're just like your father."
"Well, you've always been the sensitive one." "She's the pretty one; I'm the smart one."

We think we're being realistic, honest, or even funny. But our subconscious doesn't care about tone or intention—it cares about repetition. We lay another brick in our walk path whenever we say these phrases.

We don't just believe what we think—we begin to live what we say.

Without realizing it, our words become self-fulfilling prophecies.

But here's the shift: the same mouth that curses your future can bless it.

If language can limit, it can also **liberate**.

If words can wound, they can also **restore**.

Imagine how different life feels when you begin to speak like this:

"I haven't figured it out yet—but I'm getting there."
"I deserve joy, even when it feels unfamiliar."
"Let me try another way—I believe there's a solution."
"That was unfamiliar, but I'm proud of how I showed up."
"I see the light in you, and I trust the light in me."

Words like these don't just create better days—they cultivate a richer inner world. They soothe your nervous system, shift your perception, and provide your brain with new instructions for the path you choose to walk.

Imagine you just bombed a job interview. Instead of saying, 'I blew it,' you pause and reframe with, 'I'm learning how to show up more fully each time.' That shift is significant.

So the next time you feel tempted to say, *"I can't..." or "I always..." or "That's just me..."*

—pause.

Ask yourself:

"Is this a command I want my brain to follow?" "Is this a story I want my life to reflect?"

Because what you speak is sacred.

It shapes not only how you experience life but also how others perceive *you*.

Speak with awareness.

Let your words be deliberate.

Speak as if your words create worlds—because they do.

One Word Can Change Everything

The Ripple Effect of Loving Speech

If this feels challenging for you, do it for someone else.

Do it for the child who hears you.
Do it for the friend who needs hope.

Do it for the stranger you may never meet but who will feel the ripple of your healing words.

They don't disappear. They anchor light in places you'll never see. They nourish someone else's courage.

By choosing loving words, you lay your stone in the foundation of a new world built on truth, compassion, and healing.

Here, at this moment, in your ordinary language, everything may lie.

Your internal **map of meaning**—your dictionary of life—is shaped by language, upbringing, beliefs, and cultural codes. Every word you hear is filtered through this internal map, which is why different people can hear the same sentence but understand it entirely differently.

Your Internal Map: The Story You Tell Yourself

Your internal map is like a GPS—coded by past routes, assumptions, and warnings. Sometimes, it needs an update.

Have you ever noticed how two people can experience the same event but remember it differently?

That's because memory isn't a recording; it's a retelling—a **story you update every time you recall it**. Each time you replay a memory, your brain edits the script a little, adding new emotions and perspectives.

This means that what you call **"truth"** is just a **subjective narrative**, a dominant story you tell yourself about life. The *HeartMath Institute* even discovered that the heart has its own neurons and receives information before the brain does! In other words, *your heart "knows" before your brain processes the data.*

Every moment of your day is driven by desire and action— whether grabbing your morning coffee, checking social media, or pursuing a life-changing dream. You're always responding to an inner need, shaping your reality as you go.

But what happens when you stop and question the script? When you ask:

"Is this my truth, or is it just a hand-me-down belief?"

Reflection: The Power of Your Words

Take a few quiet moments to do a gentle *word audit*.

This isn't about guilt—it's about awareness. Bring curiosity, not judgment.

Step 1: What do you often say to yourself?

Write down three phrases you say regularly—especially in moments of stress, failure, or self-doubt.

Ask yourself:

"Are these words supporting my growth?"
"Would I say these exact words to someone I love?"

Step 2: What do you say to others?

Reflect on your words to those around you—your partner, children, friends, or coworkers.

Do you use habitual words that could limit, label, or wound?

Ask yourself:

"What would it feel like to speak encouragement instead?"
"What healing might begin just by changing one phrase?"

Step 3: Reframe with love

Take each limiting phrase and gently rewrite it. For example:

"I'm terrible at this." → *"I'm learning something new each time."*
"You never listen." → *"Can we slow down and hear each other?"*
"That's just how I am." → *"I'm open to evolving into who I truly am."*
"You never help with anything." → *"I need support—can we share the load?"*
"I'm a terrible parent." → *"I'm learning how to show up with love, even when it's hard."*

Visual Mantra: Post it, Print it, Practice it

"Every word I speak shapes a world. Let mine be a world of love."

You can write this on a sticky note, save it as your phone background, or place it somewhere visible to remind you:

When you feel rushed
When you feel harsh
When you forget your power

Sometimes, everything changes when you simply remember:
Your words are sacred.

Use them to build the life—and world—you believe in.

A Prayer for the Words We Speak

May my words be rooted in truth and rise in kindness.

May they soften pain, awaken hope, and restore what is forgotten. May I speak to myself with the love I long to hear from others.

And may my voice, however quiet, become part of the healing that this world longs for. Let my language be light.

Let my thoughts become medicine. Let my speech guide my soul home. Amen.

And so it is.

Seal this message in your heart and carry it forward.

7 Days, One You: A Loving Reset for Mind and Heart

A Structured Approach to Unlocking Whole-Brain Potential Are you ready to unlock your mind's full potential?

This seven-day brain-balancing plan integrates creativity and logic, allowing you to enhance both hemispheres of your brain. These exercises will help you think holistically, create more freely, and solve problems with clarity.

Dive in and experience the transformation!

DAY 1: Quantum Thinking & Cinematic Storytelling

Goal: Merge logic with creative imagination.

- **Exercise:** Take a complex concept (e.g., time, consciousness, emotions) and turn it into a visual story.
- **Right Brain:** Imagine it as a cinematic scene (What does time look like? How do emotions move?)
- **Left Brain:** Break it down logically—what causes it, how does it work, what are the patterns?
- **Bonus:** Act out the concept as a monologue, letting your intuition and reasoning blend.
- **Best for:** Writers, filmmakers, scientists, and philosophers.
- **Ideal Time:** Morning—fresh cognitive energy fuels both creativity and logic.

DAY 2: Improvisation & Structured Expression

Goal: Learn to balance intuition and discipline in communication.

- **Exercise:** Perform an improvised speech or monologue with two variations:
- **First Round:** Free-flow, no structure—pure emotion and impulse.
- **Second Round:** Add logical order (Intro → Problem → Solution → Conclusion).
- **Bonus Writing Task:** Write freely for 5 minutes, then restructure it into an argument or persuasive essay.
- **Ideal Time:** Afternoon—creative energy peaks while logical focus is still strong.

DAY 3: Dual Mind Mapping for Business, Research, & Creative Work

Goal: Integrate structured planning with abstract thought.

- **Exercise:** Choose a personal or work-related idea and mind-map it in two ways:
- **Left Brain:** List facts, data, categories, and logical steps.
- **Right Brain:** Explore connections using metaphors, sketches, and symbols.
- **Bonus:** Create a dialogue between a rational thinker and an intuitive dreamer debating the idea.

- **Ideal Time:** Late morning—high cognitive function helps merge creativity and structure.

DAY 4: Financial Strategy & Artistic Flow

Goal: Train the brain to shift between precision and free-flow expression.

- **Logic Exercise:** Plan a budget, investment, or business model, focusing on numbers and data.
- **Creative Counterbalance:** Immediately afterward, paint, dance, or compose something with no structure—just pure flow.
- **Connection Challenge:** Find hidden links between structured planning and creative expansion (e.g., how does a good business model mirror nature's organic patterns?).
- **Ideal Time:** Early afternoon—focused thinking followed by intuitive expansion.

DAY 5: Multisensory Exploration for Brain Synchronization

Goal: Enhance perception by stimulating both hemispheres simultaneously.

- **Exercise:** Blindfold yourself for 15 minutes and try to navigate a room, engaging other senses.

- **Bonus Sound Experiment:** Listen to music and describe it using only colors, textures, and geometric shapes.
- **Breathing Hack:** Practice alternate nostril breathing for neural balance.
- **Ideal Time:** Evening—relaxing and rewiring the brain before sleep.

DAY 6: Dream Activation & Embodied Acting

Goal: Tap into subconscious insights and express them consciously.

- **Before Sleep:** Set an intention to dream about a specific problem, goal, or idea.
- **Morning:** Write down the dream and analyze it.
- **Left Brain:** Logical interpretation (patterns, symbols, meaning). Right Brain: Intuitive/symbolic interpretation.
- **Bonus:** Act out or dramatize elements of your dream through movement or expression.
- **Ideal Time:** Night + Morning—maximizing dream recollection.

DAY 7: Future Projection & Neural Synchronization

Goal: Merge visionary thinking with strategic execution.

- **Exercise:** Imagine yourself ten years into the future—the best version of yourself.
- **Right Brain:** Visualize and feel yourself in that future reality. Left Brain: Outline the practical steps to get there.
- **Bonus:** Perform breathwork and meditation to sync both hemispheres before journaling insights.
- **Ideal Time:** Morning or sunset—perfect for expansive thinking.

Daily Mini-Routines (5-Minute Brain Hacks)

These quick brain exercises can be done daily for instant integration. Each one acts as a "micro-reset" for your mind, training both hemispheres in balance:

- **Mind Switching Drill** – Toggle between imagination and logic. Spend three minutes thinking only in images, then three minutes verbalizing ideas logically.
- **Bilingual Creativity** – Expand your communication pathways by switching languages. Express a thought in two different languages (or speech styles), activating both logic and expression.
- **Ambidextrous Challenge** – Enhance your brain's flexibility through the body. Write or brush your teeth with your non-dominant hand to strengthen neural plasticity.

- **Role Reversal** – Broaden empathy and perspective. Debate a topic from both sides, switching viewpoints mid-discussion.

Results: Whole-Brain Mastery

By the end of the seven days, you will:

Expand creative insights while enhancing structured thinking. Communicate more effectively, integrating emotion and logic. Develop new neural pathways for improved decision-making.

Holistically improve your business, artistic, and research skills.

Bringing It All Together: Your Mind Is Designing Your Masterpiece

You now understand three powerful truths: Your brain works in complementary halves. Your words shape your reality. And your beliefs—often inherited—guide your direction. Together, they create the blueprint of your mind.

Your mind is not just a tool; it's a living, breathing ecosystem, a dynamic force that responds to and actively shapes the world.

Your **brain** is your command center, processing every input, making decisions, generating responses, and storing memories like precious (or not-so-precious) files. It's the hardware of your consciousness, compelling and endlessly adaptable.

Your **language**—the words you speak to others, especially to yourself—is not just communication. It constructs the framework of your reality. Every sentence, belief, and silent inner whisper becomes a thread in the fabric of your perception.

And your **internal map**? That's your GPS—your navigation system creating the blueprint of your mind. Past experiences, early conditioning, culture, trauma, and triumphs shape it. It tells you where danger lies, where home feels safe, what success looks like, and whether you believe you deserve it.

Here's the challenge:

Most people never update their maps. They're following outdated routes programmed years ago by unkind voices, unfair systems, and beliefs that no longer serve them.

What if you could recalibrate?

Journal Prompt:

What if you paused long enough to ask:

- Is this belief mine or inherited?
- Is my language helping or harming me?
- Is this pattern serving who I am becoming?

Here's the invitation:

Unlock the vast, often hidden potential of your mind—the awareness that exists *beyond* the noise of thought, beyond inherited stories, beyond fear-based logic.

Awaken the *observer* within you—the part that doesn't just react but *creates*.

Speak a new language, one of self-trust, possibility, and conscious design.

Chart a map that aligns with your present truth, not your past pain.

Because your mind is not a fixed machine; it's a masterpiece in progress.

With love, attention, and intention, it becomes your greatest ally in building the life you came here to live.

Now that you understand how your mind operates—how you think and speak and how your inner map shapes your world—there's one thing we must face honestly: a core force—often invisible yet profoundly influential—that can hold you back from starting, evolving, and creating.

It's not a lack of talent.
It's not the world outside you.
It's not even failure.
It's something far more personal and powerful.

In the next chapter, we'll uncover a surprising inner saboteur—one that hides behind logic, perfectionism, or self-doubt—and learn how to face it with grace.

Let's explore what that is—so it never holds you back again.

CHAPTER 3
Born Without Limits

Fear—The Great Illusionist

Fear is that overdramatic friend who gasps when you trip over nothing and insists you'll fail before you even begin. It's not truth—it's a reflex. But you can change the script. We've all been there—standing at the edge of an opportunity, staring into the unknown, only to feel fear whisper, *'Better not. What if it all goes wrong?'* But remember, it's your mind creating this fear, and you have the power to control it.

Now, recall the last time fear held you back. It could be applying for that dream job, starting a passion project, or telling someone how you feel. That moment when your heart said *yes!* But your mind panicked and hit the emergency brakes. Fear isn't real—it's a sneaky mental construction designed to keep you *"safe."* Safe from what? Growth? Love? That bold, brilliant version of you who dares to try?

Fear Is Just a Thought: A Conquerable Barrier to Potential

Fear is just a thought—like when you are convinced a monster is under your bed, only to find it's just your laundry pile. It originates in the mind as a perception rather than an absolute reality. In other words, fear is a professional overthinker, always imagining the worst-case scenario as if auditioning for a dramatic role. Stoic philosophers like Marcus Aurelius recognized this and advised us to stop giving fear the lead role in our lives.

Fear operates like a shadow: it appears terrifying until you realize it's your exaggerated reaction to the unknown. It feeds on false assumptions, limiting beliefs, and those ridiculous stories we tell ourselves—like how *one* awkward moment at a party means we should never socialize again.

According to cognitive behavioral therapy (CBT), fear is often fueled by distorted thinking, meaning your brain is a prankster playing tricks on you. Neuroscientists support this, showing that while fear originates in the amygdala (the drama queen of the brain), your prefrontal cortex (the logical adult) can tell it to calm down.

The key to overcoming fear begins with this realization: just because a thought appears in your mind doesn't mean it deserves your attention. Thoughts are like spam emails—most can be deleted without response.

Marcus Aurelius, the Stoic emperor, reminded us: *"You have power over your mind—not outside events."* His wisdom teaches that fear is simply a misuse of imagination, and by mastering our inner dialogue, we reclaim control over life's stage.

Jean-Paul Sartre, the existentialist, added another dimension: fear is not proof of weakness but the anxiety of freedom. Every choice carries weight, and with that weight comes unease. But Sartre urges us to see this anxiety as the price of freedom, not proof of failure.

Then comes Viktor Frankl, who endured the horrors of a concentration camp and still chose his response. His lesson is timeless: while we cannot always choose our circumstances, we can always choose our attitude toward them. If Frankl could find meaning in the darkest places, surely we can face the stage, the blank page, or the vulnerable conversation that stands before us.

Modern psychology echoes these insights. Cognitive Behavioral Therapy (CBT) shows that fear often springs from distorted thinking—the mind exaggerating danger like a prankster in disguise. Neuroscience confirms this, revealing that while fear sparks in the amygdala, the prefrontal cortex has the power to say, "Calm down. Let's think this through."

The takeaway is clear: fear is not the enemy. It is the invitation. And your choices—moment by moment—are the keys to your freedom.

The truth? Most of what we fear isn't even real. It's a memory, a what-if, a ghost in the hallway.

The cage door has always been open because, plot twist, there was never an actual cage. It was all in your head—like a psychological escape room where the only thing keeping you trapped is forgetting to turn the metaphorical doorknob. Buddhists figured this out ages ago, teaching that fear is just an illusion and mindfulness is the key to seeing through it. Once you understand this, you'll feel a profound sense of relief and peace, knowing that fear is not a real threat but a mental construct you can overcome.

What's the moral of the story?

Fear and self-doubt are like those overly dramatic reality TV contestants—entertaining but not to be taken seriously. You regain your power when you realize fear is just a thought, not a truth. The cage door has always been open— you just have to walk through it. And if you need an extra push, imagine Marcus Aurelius facepalming every time you let fear stop you.

From Panic to Peace

This is how I handle fear. A few days ago, I discovered a message in my garbage can: *"You are not alone. 5/1 5/2."*

Stalker? My mind raced with worst-case scenarios. But then another thought emerged: *"Oh, indeed, I am not alone. I have always believed in the presence of others in my life. I love people, my neighbors, and having them around me."* What a comforting realization! I installed cameras—not out of panic, but from a sense of empowerment. I didn't freeze; I continued with my daily routine. Fear didn't overwhelm me; I took control.

Fear is the mind's outdated security system, designed to keep you within the familiar. It thrives in the subconscious, recycling past failures and societal conditioning until the unknown feels threatening. However, these limits are self-imposed—and breaking through them is essential for transformation. The unknown isn't your enemy; it's a gateway to growth.

The key to moving beyond fear lies in trusting your inner voice. When we truly listen to it, fear dissipates. This inner voice will protect and propel us forward when it knows we are ready to leap.

Breaking the Fear Loop

Identifying the Root Causes of Fear

Fear often stems from past experiences, societal expectations, or the ego's desperate need for control. Labeling your fears weakens their grip. Instead of saying, *"I'm afraid of failure,"* try, *"I have a thought that I might fail, but I don't have to believe it."* Changing your language shifts your perception.

The Science Behind Overcoming Self-Doubt

Studies show that the brain rewires itself through repetition and intention. Fear pathways can be overridden by action. Each time you take a risk, your brain learns that the world doesn't collapse when you step outside your comfort zone.

Tools for Building Genuine Self-Confidence

- **Micro-Risks:** Try something new, speak up, or take a different route.
- **Reframing:** Replace "What if I fail?" with "What if I soar?"
- **Future You Exercise:** Ask your future self for guidance on what to do today.

Overcoming Shyness and Claiming What You Deserve

You may hesitate to step forward—not due to incapacity, but because you've been conditioned to believe you don't deserve more. Whether it's shyness, impostor syndrome, or fear of rejection, these limiting beliefs often originate from childhood experiences.

- **What if this isn't true?** Imagine being in a relationship where you deeply love your partner but fear expressing your true needs. You hesitate to ask for more time together, more affection, or to voice your concerns. Why? Because deep down, you fear rejection or being *"too much."* But here's the truth: **Your wants and needs are valid.** Holding back breeds stagnation and resentment.

Eureka moment: The next time you find yourself suppressing your truth, remind yourself: **Vulnerability fosters deeper connections, not rejection.** When you trust your inner voice and express your truth, fear vanishes, and you open the door to authentic relationships.

They eventually say, 'I need more time with you.' Instead of rejection, they respond with warmth, deepening your connection.

The Freedom Found in Embracing Vulnerability

Vulnerability isn't weakness—it's the birthplace of courage. When you stop fearing judgment and embrace your authentic self, life unfolds in unimaginable ways.

Stories of Transformation

My Journey: From Fear to Freedom

My transformation began slowly—first with small choices, then bold ones. It didn't happen overnight, but it did happen.

Before my awakening, fear dictated much of my life. Oh dear, it was buried so deeply that it morphed into silent anger, suffocating me daily. I wandered through misery, unaware of its source or the weight I carried. Yet, the vulnerability of being both a mentor and a human is a gift. It requires the courage to confront ignorance and seek the truth. Growth is not optional—you must embrace personal wisdom every day. This is your responsibility to those you guide, but more importantly, it's your proof that we are all in this together. If one person can do it, so can you.

Reflecting on my journey, I played roles that weren't mine, following a script written by others—society, expectations, and outdated beliefs. Breaking free meant leaving behind the safety net of familiarity. It meant facing financial struggles, raising my children alone, and navigating an ultra-competitive industry in America.

Why step away from safety? From the beauty, warmth, incredible food, and the Aegean Sea of Greece?

Yes, I miss my friends, the flavors, the laughter, my parents. But I no longer fear. Most importantly, I no longer carry anger. I am free. I changed direction and followed my path. Obstacles will always exist—sometimes towering, making you think, *"I can't leap this time; it's too far."* But with patience, wisdom arrives each day. Hidden joy resides within every challenge. It's the paradox of life—the balance of being both a responsible adult and a wild, joyful child racing across the court, daring to play. And in the end, scoring.

The journey is worthwhile. The transformation is a blessing. The *"old you"* becomes part of your growth and a distant memory. People say you change. I say you don't change—you evolve. Evolution means gifting yourself new lenses and seeing the world with a clearer, more advanced perspective. Do not fear those who feel safer with your old glasses—they cling to the past, afraid of the unknown. You have upgraded. As you rise, they may fade from your life. That, too, is part of the gift.

The Beauty of Risk-Taking

Taking risks is like jumping into the ocean. Initially, it's cold and shocking, but soon you feel alive. You'll never achieve different outcomes by thinking the same way. Growth demands discomfort. Every great leap begins with a frightening step.

Real People Who Faced Fear:

- **Oprah:** Fired early. Built her own empire.

- **Rowling:** Rejected twelve times. Changed the world anyway.

Oprah Winfrey was fired from her first television job and told she was *"unfit for TV."* Instead of succumbing to fear, she used it as fuel to create her own space—becoming one of the most influential media moguls of all time.

When she wrote Harry Potter, J.K. Rowling was a struggling single mother living on welfare. Twelve publishers rejected her manuscript, but she didn't let fear deter her. She believed in her story, and eventually, the world did.

What do they share in common?

They refused to let fear dictate their decisions.

How to Overcome Fear and Limitations

Fear Is Fiction: The Story You Don't Have to Tell Anymore

Fear is a construct—an illusion that can be dismantled, allowing your true potential to shine. It is a conditioned response, a mental habit. The good news? **Habits can be changed.** The next time fear knocks, don't let it in—acknowledge it, thank it for trying to *"protect"* you, and move forward anyway.

The "Thank You, But No Thank You" Exercise

When fear arises, instead of resisting or suppressing it, acknowledge it:

- *Say internally, "Thank you for trying to protect me, but I don't need you right now."*
- *Visualize yourself stepping through it like mist dissolving behind you.*
- *Shift your focus to an empowering thought that reminds you of your strength.*

Fear Exposure Challenge

Fear loses power when confronted. Choose one small thing you avoid due to fear and do it:

- *Afraid of public speaking? Contribute to a group conversation.*
- *Fear of rejection? Smile at strangers.*
- *Fear of failure? Start a creative project without pressure for perfection.*

Each small step teaches your brain that fear is an illusion.

Envision Your Future Self

- *Close your eyes and visualize your highest self—fearless, confident, limitless.*
- *Ask your future version: "What would you tell me about this fear?"*

- *Trust this forgotten inner voice. Let the answers arise naturally.*

Change Your Physiology

Fear is not just mental; it's physical. Change your state:

- *Breathe deeply—Inhale for 4 seconds, hold for 4, and exhale for 8. Focus solely on your breathing.*
- *Move—Exercise, dance, and shake it out. Fear cannot survive in an empowered body.*
- *Smile—Yes, even when you don't feel like it. Your brain will respond.*

Act "As If"

Act as if you're already fearless:

- *Walk, speak, and move like someone who has no limitations.*
- *Make decisions from the mindset of someone who believes in themselves completely.*
- *Your mind will catch up to your actions.*

Freedom List

- *Write down what you gain by moving past that fear.*
- *Let your desire for freedom outweigh your attachment to fear.*
- *Enrich the list daily; every small detail contributes to significant change.*

The Ultimate Tool: Reframe Your Fear

Fear often stems from the narratives we create.

Do you understand the distinction between writing and narrating a story about yourself?

The difference lies in the depth of impact, how your subconscious processes it, and how it shapes your identity.

Writing Solidifies Reality

Writing carries a unique, energetic imprint—once something is written down, it becomes tangible, almost like a contract with your subconscious. That's why it's essential to avoid writing negative beliefs, as they can reinforce limitations rather than dissolve them. Writing serves as intentional programming for the mind.

- *When you write your truth (e.g., "I am fearless and limitless"), your subconscious starts to accept it as reality.*
- *If you record fears and doubts, they become anchors, solidifying those emotions in your psyche.*
- *Writing clarifies thoughts and commits you to a new mindset.*

Speaking Shapes Perception

Narrating a story about yourself, whether aloud or internally, is fluid—it allows for evolution but also carries subconscious emotional weight.

- *If you consistently tell a disempowering story (e.g., "I always fail at relationships" or "I'm not lucky"), you* reinforce that belief, leading your mind to seek evidence to support it.

- Conversely, if you share an empowering story ("I am constantly learning and growing in love and life"), you reshape your reality and how others perceive you.
- Stories shape your emotional body, while writing engraves them into your mental framework.

The Power of Speaking vs. Writing

- Speaking creates a momentary vibration—it influences emotions in real-time.
- Writing makes it permanent—it imprints a new identity blueprint in your subconscious.
- Combining both facilitates a full-circle transformation: write your power and speak it into existence.

How to Use Both for Growth

Write only empowering truths. Place them around your home, journal them, and allow them to reshape your subconscious.

Tell a better story about yourself. When reflecting on your past, reframe challenges as stepping stones, not barriers.

Speak your affirmations aloud after writing them. The vibration of your voice reinforces your truth.

See them. Touch them. Smell them. Taste them. Speak them. Hear them.

Become them.

You are not your *fear*. You are your evolution.

Your words create worlds. Be mindful of what you choose to write and say—you shape your future with every thought, sentence, and belief.

Your Story is Your Power

That moment when you realized there's more to life than fear? That was your true self speaking. Fear will always attempt to confine you, but now you understand the truth—it holds no power unless you grant it power. Fear is a construct you can dismantle, allowing your true potential to shine. It's merely a conditioned response, a mental habit.

The good news?

Habits can be changed.

You're not just moving beyond fear—you're stepping into authorship. In the next chapter, we'll explore how rewriting your story reshapes your destiny.

Ready to step into your power?

CHAPTER 4
Embracing Your Story

Your Life, Your Script

Imagine your life as a novel, where each morning you write a new page. Some days bring unexpected twists, while others feel like drama or comedy—but you hold the pen.

Now, consider this: if your life were a movie, would you be the protagonist or merely an extra in someone else's story? Would you be the hero facing challenges or a background character observing life unfold? The truth is, the more you own your story, the more powerful and fulfilled you become.

To be powerful means to be loved by the one person who truly matters—yourself. When you love yourself, you cease to seek validation and start living in alignment.

Self-love isn't about arrogance; it's about embracing yourself with kindness, recognizing your worth, and accepting all parts of you—even those you once deemed unlovable. When you cultivate love within, you become a gift to the world, empowering yourself to take control of your life.

High-frequency emotions like love, empathy, gratitude, and acceptance are transformative forces. They can shape your reality, influence your environment, and uplift those around you. Cultivating these positive emotions is an act of self-liberation, a choice to shift your energy toward a more hopeful and optimistic future.

Be mindful of your thoughts and experiences.

Use your free will to transform the low frequency of negative emotions into the high frequency of gratitude and unconditional love. Establish a sense of empowerment, embodied strength, and kindness.

That's the real you—undeniably authentic and, fortunately for everyone, delightfully easy to embrace!

You are not defined by your past. You are the limitless potential of who you are becoming.

Stay mindful. You can shape your future to be as bright and healthy as possible.

Powerlessness, helplessness, feeling trapped, immobilized, defeated, despaired, fearful—these emotions stem from thoughts rooted in the past, thoughts you have adapted as behaviors. But you are not your past, behaviors, or fleeting emotions.

You are you.

Take a moment to recall instances when you positively influenced others, whether in your family, friendships, or business. Reflect on leadership moments, acts of kindness, and decisions that elevated your energy. Let these memories remind you of your impact. Allow the feeling of empowerment to intensify in your mind, heart, and body.

Now, visualize that powerful feeling expanding within you.

1. Recall a time you uplifted someone.
2. Breathe into that feeling.
3. Visualize it spreading through your body.
4. Let it rise to your mind's eye.
5. Remember this sensation throughout your day.

Your story is still unfolding, and you control how your next moment, day, week, or year begins.

Your Story is Your Superpower.

Your personal story holds the power to redefine and elevate your existence. The more consciously you engage with it, the more successful and mature you become. Spiritual maturity allows you to synchronize with the power of your thoughts.

What you think about most, you become.

You are not just a passive observer of life—you are the creator of who you choose to be. You can make a new choice at any moment, shift your behaviors, and take control of your narrative. This realization should inspire and motivate you to start writing a new, empowering chapter in your life.

Nobody has a say in this but you.

Life: The Ultimate DIY Movie

Oliver Sacks, the neurologist famous for making the human mind sound like an adventure novel, once said:

"You're the director and the lead. The story is yours to tell, scene by scene."

Translation? You're not merely living the movie—you're also directing it. And good news? You can reshoot the next scene.

Consider this: every choice you make, every regrettable email you send, every dance move you pull off (or don't) at a wedding shapes your story. But here's the twist—who's watching? Who's the one inside your head observing all this chaos unfold?

That's your consciousness—your inner observer, the "you" beyond the roles you play. It's the part of you that doesn't care if you wear sweatpants at 3 p.m. or give a TED Talk at 8 p.m. It's simply *aware*. That awareness is tied to how you perceive yourself. If you start thinking of yourself as bold and fearless, guess what? You'll start living that way.

But hold onto your popcorn—it gets even stranger. Life isn't as linear as we think. Imagine a film reel. Every scene already exists, but you experience them one frame at a time. Past, present, and future swirl around in some cosmic waiting room, and you get to choose which scene to step into next. Time feels linear, but change isn't. You can alter your 'timeline' anytime by choosing a new belief or direction.

So, what's the takeaway? You're not just the *actor* in your life—you're the *director, writer, editor,* and sometimes the *special effects technician* trying to clean up the mess. The good news? You can rewrite scenes, change the script, and give yourself a better ending anytime.

Now, go direct something epic.

Rewriting Your Narrative

We all carry stories—some we wrote, some written for us. Often inherited from family, culture, or past experiences, these narratives dictate how we see ourselves and the world.

Maybe you grew up hearing:

"Money doesn't grow on trees."
"Be realistic. Dreaming big only leads to disappointment."
"Love always ends in pain."

At first, these phrases seem harmless—just words. But when repeated often enough, they become mental blueprints that shape your beliefs, decisions, and reality.

Here's the truth: just because a story was handed to you doesn't mean you have to keep reading from the same script. Your life isn't a fixed novel written in ink—it's a screenplay still in progress. And the best part? You hold the pen.

Ever caught yourself thinking:

"I'm always unlucky."
"I'm too old to start over."
"People like me don't succeed."

Hold on. Who planted those thoughts in your mind? Was it someone who sees you clearly and objectively? Someone thriving in their own life, fulfilled and successful? And more importantly, why are you still carrying their baggage as your truth?

These are just old scripts—outdated, uninspired, and frankly, *not entertaining.* You wouldn't watch a movie where the main character never grows, never overcomes obstacles, and never surprises the audience. So why live one?

Your story isn't fixed—it's evolving. And this moment is your cue to turn the page.

How to Build a Narrative of Empowerment

Flip the Script

Whenever a limiting belief arises, challenge it:

- Instead of *"I'm terrible with money,"*→ Try *"I'm learning to make smarter financial decisions daily, and it's paying off."*
- Instead of *"I always fail,"*→ Try *"Every challenge is a stepping stone to my success."*

- Instead of *"He doesn't feel attracted to me anymore,"* → Try *"Our connection continues to evolve, bringing new layers of attraction and depth."*
- Instead of *"After we had kids, she doesn't care for herself,"* → Try *"Motherhood has added a unique glow to her, and I admire how she embraces it."*
- Instead of *"I'm too late to pivot,"* → Try *"I bring wisdom and fresh perspective to every new chapter."*

Your brain loves repetition, so feed it a better story.

Create a Character Arc

Imagine you are the protagonist of your film. What would your character's journey look like?

What challenges must you overcome?
How can you transform your weaknesses into your greatest strengths? What strengths must you develop?
How does the final act transform you?

You're not a background extra in someone else's movie. You are the main character—so act like it.

Daily Editing

Every morning, take a moment to "write" your day as if it were a fresh page in your book.

How do you want to feel?
What actions will move your story forward?
What chapter are you stepping into today?

What thoughts will elevate your day and set the tone for happiness?

The more intentionally you set the stage, the more powerful your story becomes.

From Pain to Power: Using the Past to Fuel the Future

Your past isn't an anchor—it's fuel.

Everything you've endured—the heartbreak, the failures, the rejections—has prepared you for what's next. But only if you use it wisely.

Consider this well-known example:

Two brothers grew up in the same home, raised by a violent, alcoholic father. They endured the same chaos, the same fear, and the same scars. Yet, their paths diverged as they grew older. One became a doctor of discipline, compassion, and healing. He used his painful past as motivation to help others, break the cycle, and become the person he never had growing up. The other followed in his father's footsteps—drowning in alcohol, lashing out in violence, trapped in the very cycle he once despised. He saw his past as a curse, a reason he could never be more. When asked, *"Why did you choose this path?"* they both answered the same way: *"Because of my father."*

Same upbringing. Same pain. Two completely different choices.

A Real-Life Rewrite: The Story of Resilience

Returning to my own story, I have a wonderful mother. Her greatest dream was to live in the United States of America. She traveled there countless times, often taking me with her. I witnessed how her eyes lit up when she spoke about this dream, how she felt at home in a land she never fully claimed.

But life offers choices, and during her lifetime, she made decisions that prevented her from staying. She never fulfilled her dream, and to this day, she carries that regret.

I held onto the same dream: to move to the States, and I did it.

This was not just a relocation—it was a reinvention, a conscious decision to rewrite the narrative that had unfolded before me. My mother chose to stay, while I chose to step into a life that wasn't meant for me, according to my inherited story. But stories can change.

It was the bravest decision of my life. It's not the easiest, but it was the most enlightened. If I hadn't rewritten my story, I wouldn't be here talking to you right now.

I started saying *yes* to opportunities. I made different choices. I didn't just remain an artist—I became an educator and researcher. I stepped onto stages as a speaker. I wrote my second, third, and fourth books. I shaped success on my terms. I built a movement around my message.

The people who once called me "quiet" now see me as a force of nature.

I didn't change *who I am*—I changed the story about who I am. And that changed everything.

What story in your lineage is asking for a rewrite? What chapter are you meant to complete differently?

The Story of Others Who Rewrote Their Lives

Trevor Noah grew up in apartheid South Africa, where his very existence was considered illegal. Instead of letting that define him, he used humor, storytelling, and resilience to become one of the world's most influential comedians.

Sara Blakely was selling fax machines door-to-door when she had an idea: footless pantyhose. People laughed. Banks rejected her. But she rewrote her story, persisted, and built Spanx—now a billion-dollar brand.

Andrea Bocelli was told he'd never succeed in music because of his blindness. It's fortunate he didn't listen—his voice has moved millions worldwide.

These individuals weren't born extraordinary. They became extraordinary by refusing to let fear or old narratives limit them—and so can you.

What do they have in common? They chose their narrative instead of letting others write it for them.

Your Story Shapes Your Reality

You're not stuck in a script you didn't write. You're the architect now—the one who chooses the words, the meaning, the direction. What will your next chapter reveal?

Stuck in a chapter you don't like? Write a new one.
Regretting a past decision? Turn it into a lesson.
Afraid of the unknown? Make it an adventure.

Everything you believe about yourself—your worth, your potential—is a story you tell yourself.

Why not make it a legendary one?

Now that you understand the power of your story, it's time to take it a step further. Who are you truly meant to be? What purpose is waiting to unfold within you? How do you step into your most fulfilled, powerful self?

In the next chapter, we dive deep into discovering and living your purpose.

Ready?

CHAPTER 5
Aligning with Your Purpose

Living Your Purpose Now

Every day begins with routine: brushing your teeth, making coffee, checking your phone. But what if these moments—these rituals—could become something more? Not just automatic, but intentional. Not just practical, but meaningful.

Much of life involves moving from one task to the next, but what if each action carried an intention beyond the practical? Waking up wouldn't just be about starting another day—it would be an opportunity to greet the morning with clarity and purpose. Whether you're brushing your teeth, tying your shoes, or making coffee, each act can become sacred when done with intention. These aren't just tasks; they are daily invitations to embody purpose.

Small, repetitive moments that seem ordinary can hold extraordinary significance when approached with awareness. When you tie your shoes, you're not just getting ready to leave the house—you're preparing to step into the world with direction and intention. When you eat, you're not just consuming food—you're nourishing your body, fueling your energy, and honoring the life that sustains you. Even something as simple as writing an email becomes an act of impact, shaping connections and sharing thoughts with purpose. For instance, when you write an email, you can do it to foster understanding or provide support, infusing even this mundane task with meaning.

Life is not just a collection of tasks driven by reasons; it is a continuous unfolding of moments, each carrying the potential for meaning. When you shift from simply *doing* to truly *experiencing*, you align your daily actions with something more significant. Purpose is not found in a distant, grand achievement—it is woven into how you live, breathe, and move through the world. Every small act can reflect who you are and who you are becoming. The question is, will you live by routine, or will you live with purpose?

Finding Purpose: Where Passion Meets Clarity

You are not here by accident. That's not just a comforting thought—it's the truth. You were born with a purpose that no one can define. It's not something you need to chase or force; it already exists within you. If you ever feel lost, purpose has a way of revealing itself. It speaks through your dreams and aspirations, the kindness you show, and the powerful ideas you hold—like the one that visits you in the quiet before sleep or whispers when you're moved by a stranger's kindness. Everything that makes you, *you* is part of why you are here.

Right now, stop everything else and focus. Let go of distractions. Align with that deep knowing inside you because your purpose needs you. It's the reason behind everything else you do, the energy that drives you forward. Every small action in your life—every task, responsibility, or routine—should ultimately connect back to it.

Alignment isn't just passion—it's clarity. It's that feeling when time disappears, when effort feels natural, when decisions feel right even in fear. Misalignment? That's when life feels heavy and unclear.

Pause here.

Are you consciously choosing your purpose?

Or unconsciously following someone else's?

If you stop searching for purpose in grand, distant moments and start seeing it in the life you are already living, you'll realize it has been there all along. It is woven into your breath, thoughts, choices, and actions. It's not a future destination—it's the path you are walking right now. So, instead of rushing through the day, **slow down.** Instead of viewing life as a collection of tasks, see it as **a series of meaningful moments.** Instead of believing your purpose is separate from your daily life, start living as if **every step you take is already part of it**.

Because it is.

What It Means to "Find" Your Purpose

Purpose doesn't always arrive like a lightning bolt—or a fortune cookie. Sometimes it's subtle. Sometimes it's loud. But always, it's real.

Here's the thing: Purpose isn't found by overthinking. It reveals itself through **action, reflection, and self-awareness**. It evolves as you evolve, changes as you change, and, most importantly, it requires you to **pay attention.**

The Emotional & Mental State of Alignment

Wondering if you're on the right path? Your emotions leave clues:

Feeling inspired? That's a sign. Keep going.

Feeling drained? Your soul is waving a red flag. Something's off.

Feeling lost? Congratulations! You've just received an invitation to explore.

Your emotions are GPS signals from within. Ignore them, and you risk driving in circles—or worse, getting stuck in someone else's map.

Steps to Rediscover & Connect with Your Purpose

If you've ever thought, *I don't know my purpose*, don't panic. That's like saying, *I don't know where my missing sock went*. It's still somewhere—you must look in the right places. Here's how:

Follow Curiosity. If something naturally excites you, pay attention. It's trying to tell you something.

Try Things. Overthinking won't help. Purpose isn't found in theory—it's revealed through experience.

Listen to Your Inner Voice. The more you trust yourself, the more precise your purpose becomes.

Do the Work. Passion without action is just a nice idea. Purpose requires movement.

What's one moment from this week that made you feel most alive—and why?

The Impact of Purposeful Living

Living in alignment with your purpose doesn't just make life *better*—it makes life *make sense*.

People who live with purpose don't just wake up happier; they're also more resilient, creative, and fulfilled. When you're aligned, life flows. You're not constantly fighting against the current—you're moving with it. It doesn't mean everything is effortless, but it means everything has meaning.

Want vs. Choice: Clarity Through Action

When determining what you truly desire, ask yourself:

- *Do I want to be correct, or do I want to be happy? (Hint: You can't always have both.)*
- *Are my desires spiritual, emotional, or physical? (Understanding this prevents pursuing the wrong thing.)*
- *Am I motivated by love or fear? (Fear-based decisions never lead to true fulfillment.)*
- *Is my mind trained to actively pursue what I want, or am I merely wishing? (Manifesting is great, but action is essential.)*

The Empathy Triangle: A Purposeful Way of Living

Living with purpose involves not just personal success but also how you navigate the world. The *Empathy Triangle* serves as a guide to forging more meaningful connections, which are *always* linked to purpose:

- **Cultivate curiosity about others.** *(Genuine interest fosters real connection.)*
- **Observe human nature with interest, not judgment.** *(People are stories, not stereotypes.)*

- **Exit the isolation of your ego.** *(Life is richer when it's not solely about you.)*
- **Discard labels and recognize shared humanity.** *(We're more alike than we realize.)*
- **Create shared experiences.** *(Real bonds form through common moments.)*
- **Walk in another's shoes without needing to "fix" them.** *(Empathy doesn't imply control.)*
- **Engage in radical listening.** *(I am not just waiting to speak; I am truly listening.)*
- **Choose love over judgment.** *(People aren't defined by their worst moments.)*

Your life isn't waiting to start—**it's happening right now**. Purpose isn't discovered in some future moment of clarity; it resides in your choices today. So, be present. Pay attention. And respond when purpose calls, whether through a significant life event or a fleeting thought in the middle of the night.

When Purpose Calls, Step Beyond the Familiar

My Journey of Purpose from Stage to Supraconscious

Finding your purpose often requires distancing yourself from the familiar. It demands withdrawing from the safety of what you know, what others expect, and what feels comfortable. People may say you've lost your way or that you don't know what you're doing. And perhaps, for a time, you won't. But here's the paradox—when your *mind* finds clarity, your *heart* finds peace. And when your heart is at peace, your days are filled with joy, even amidst uncertainty.

For me, the first whisper of purpose came in my sleep—a fleeting moment, just beyond my grasp. Yet, it wasn't clear. Purpose rarely arrives with a neatly packaged explanation; it reveals itself *in layers*. The true revelation came on stage during a moment of complete surrender. It was an *aha* moment, one of those rare experiences where something greater than you unfolds, and suddenly, you *feel* an infinite field of possibilities has opened before you. I didn't know what it was, but I recognized the need to explore it.

I dislike ignorance more than anything. The unknown doesn't frighten me—*not knowing* does. So I had to discover the truth. That's when the unfolding began. My purpose was guiding me even before I realized it.

It took years to understand that I was not just an actor—I was a seeker. My work for my characters wasn't merely about performance; it served as a portal to new paradigms, theories, and perspectives on what *experience* is. Through acting, I wasn't just uncovering characters—I was discovering *truths* about human nature, consciousness, and the infinite layers of existence.

It's a long story—one I've poured into my book, *Supraconscious: The Genius Within You*. That book isn't just a collection of words; it's my *mind* laid bare. It's my *purpose* articulated in language.

And that, in itself, is remarkable.

When Success Feels Empty: The Banker Who Found Purpose in Dirt and the Coder Who Chose Alpacas Over Algorithms

The Banker Who Swapped Billions for Basil

Meet Richard "Rich" Gainsworth, a powerhouse investment banker who spent decades closing multimillion-dollar deals from a high-rise office. His life epitomized Wall Street dreams—sleek cars, a penthouse with a skyline view, and an assistant dedicated to ensuring his coffee was always at the perfect temperature.

But one day, as he stared at another spreadsheet filled with soulless numbers, an unsettling thought struck him: *I've made billions but don't even know how potatoes grow.*

That realization flipped a switch in his mind. Within months, Rich did something unimaginable—he walked away from finance and bought a 100-acre farm in Vermont. His new life? Gainsworth Greens, an organic farm where he wakes up with the sun, talks to his chickens (who, unlike corporate board members, actually listen), and feels more alive than ever.

Why does this align with his purpose?

He used to predict stock trends; now he tracks tomato harvests. Where boardroom charts once dominated his view, he now sees rows of greens and goats. Purpose emerged not from more deals but from more dirt under his fingernails.

The Coder Who Switched Clicks for Connection

Say hello to Jake "Cloud" Henderson, a Silicon Valley prodigy who co-founded a prominent AI startup. He was the genius behind an algorithm that could predict your lunch choice before you even got hungry. The world lauded his innovation, but deep down, he felt *empty*.

His work revolved around making people click faster. But what about living more slowly?

After a grueling 36-hour coding marathon, he snapped. "I need fresh air. And animals. And a life where I don't receive emails at 3 AM." So, he did the unthinkable, left it all behind, and bought a ranch in Montana. Today, he raises alpacas, grows heirloom vegetables, and runs a tech-free retreat where burned-out startup founders detox from Wi-Fi and reconnect with reality.

Why This Aligns with His Purpose:

Jake's soul craved simplicity and authenticity. He transitioned from optimizing AI to optimizing *life*— learning to milk goats, making artisanal cheese, and embracing a world where "buffering" only applies to homemade butter. He still loves tech, but now, instead of tracking consumer behavior, he monitors seasons and soil health.

The lesson? Purpose isn't always where you think it is.

Rich and Jake built empires of success only to realize that success without purpose is merely an expensive illusion. The world told them they had everything, yet they *felt* like they had nothing. Their pivots weren't about abandoning ambition but redirecting it toward something that made them feel alive.

Purpose isn't always found in expected places.

Sometimes, it waits in quiet moments, in the soil, in the sunrise, or even in the eyes of a wise alpaca.

The Power You Seek Is Already Yours

Revisit that moment at the beginning of this chapter when you envisioned your highest self. That version of you is real. All you have to do is align.

You don't *find* purpose—you **live into it.**

Clarity arises from action, not thought. The more you step forward, the more your path reveals itself.

Every choice, every day, shapes your destiny.

The world doesn't need a perfect version of you. It needs the present you.

Purpose without emotional mastery can feel like riding a rocket without a navigation system. In the next chapter, we explore how to master your emotions and mind so that your purpose becomes not just a dream but a lived reality.

CHAPTER 6

Ruling The Inner Kingdom

Who's Running the Show?

Think back to a moment when an overwhelming emotion dictated your actions. Perhaps it was something significant—your child was sick, you failed an important exam, or you experienced deep heartbreak. Or maybe it was something small but equally triggering—your partner left for work without a kiss, someone cut you off in traffic, or your boss sent a curt email. The events may vary, but what's your reaction? That's where your power lies.

How you react isn't about the event but about how you structure your thoughts and emotions. And here's the truth: *You are not the storm—you're the sky that holds it.*

The moment you rein in your ego—shifting from an egocentric mindset to a healthy, self-aware one—you become the master, not the puppet, of your emotional world.

Let's be clear: Emotions are not mystical forces that randomly hijack your brain. They follow patterns, have triggers, and—here's the kicker—you can *direct* them.

That's precisely why I'm using the example of acting.

Acting is the art that *lives and breathes* emotion. If there's one group of people who know how to produce feelings on command, it's actors. They don't just feel emotions—they **create, shape, and express** them with precision.

I've spent 25 years guiding actors through the deep, unpredictable waters of the "feelings pool." I've witnessed firsthand what it takes to summon emotion and—more importantly—how to navigate it without drowning. So, if anyone can teach you how to master your feelings while fully experiencing them, it's an acting coach and an actor; it's someone like me.

The question isn't *whether* you have emotions—you do. The real question is:

Are you running the show, or are your emotions directing you like a poorly written script?

Emotions are your instruments. Learn to play them with purpose; don't let them play you.

Mastering your emotions liberates you from reactive living and unlocks creativity, insight, and success. When you gain emotional control, you don't suppress feelings; you learn to harness them.

You always have a choice:

- → Let emotions dominate you
- → Take charge of your emotions

Ruling your emotions doesn't mean becoming a detached, unfeeling robot. It means recognizing that emotions are like children on a long road trip—acknowledge them, but don't let them drive the car. Let's break it down.

Feelings vs. Emotions: What's the Difference?

Understanding the distinction between 'feelings' and 'emotions' is a powerful tool that can enlighten and empower you.

What Are Emotions?

Emotions are **raw energy.** They are immediate, instinctual reactions hardwired into your biology, arising before you even have time to think. If a bear walks into the room right now, your body will trigger fear before you can rationalize anything. Your heart will race, adrenaline will flood your system, and your muscles will tense, preparing you to fight or flee.

This is your survival mechanism in action.

Emotions are fast, powerful, and universal. No matter where you're from, you'll wince in pain if you stub your toe. If you win the lottery, you'll feel joy. If someone betrays you, anger will bubble up.

But emotions, on their own, are just **signals.** They don't last.

They're like sparks—they come and go.

What Are Feelings?

Feelings, on the other hand, are how you interpret and express those emotions.

Emotions are the raw ingredients—like flour, eggs, and sugar. Feelings are the cake you bake with them, shaped by your experiences. Add a dash of memory, a spoonful of belief—and the outcome changes entirely.

For example:

You feel **fear** *(emotion) when you hear a sudden noise at night.*
You feel **paranoia** *(feeling) when you interpret that noise as an intruder.*
You feel **relief** *(emotion) when you realize it is just the wind.*

It's important to recognize that your memories, experiences, and thoughts significantly shape your feelings. This understanding can make you more introspective and self-aware.

Like an actor tapping into memory to stir tears, you can choose your emotional lens with intention and artistry.

That's the real magic.

And that's what you can do in your own life.

The Art of Holding Your Power

Holding your emotions in check is not about suppression; it's about direction. Think of it as the difference between a river and a flood—one is controlled power, while the other is chaotic destruction. One flows through you with strength; the other destroys everything in its path. Learn to channel your emotions so they work for you, not against you.

Power isn't about dominating others—it's about mastering yourself.

- *When someone criticizes you, do you react defensively or take a deep breath and assess the truth in their words?*
- *When rejection stings, do you spiral into self-doubt or remind yourself that rejection is simply redirection?*
- *When fear whispers that you're not good enough, do you listen or respond with courage?*

The power you seek is already within you—it's just buried under layers of conditioning, fears, and unexamined beliefs. The more you consciously choose your responses, the more you reclaim your power.

Rewriting Your Emotional Script

Most people believe they're stuck with the emotions they've always had. "I've always been this way," they say. "I can't change how I feel."

That's simply **not true.**

Your emotional patterns were formed by past experiences—many of which you've long forgotten. You didn't choose them consciously; they were shaped by how your brain processed events in your life. Understanding this can help you navigate your emotional landscape more effectively.

Think of your emotional landscape as a map. Some roads were drawn by childhood experiences, some by society, some by heartbreak, and some by joy. But here's the good news: **You can redraw the map.**

If your past made you associate love with pain, you can rewrite that belief.

If rejection has paralyzed you, you can train yourself to see it as redirection. If anger has controlled you, you can learn to channel it into purpose.

Remapping your emotional memory can help you rewrite your emotional script and transform your life. This process can also give you hope and motivation for personal growth.

Instead of being a passive character in your life, you become the *writer, director, and lead role.*

Rewrite your emotional script—scene by scene. You're not stuck in your past plot. You're the storyteller now.

Wisdom from the Ancients: Odysseus and the Mastery of Self

Most people know Odysseus as the hero of *The Odyssey*, but they don't realize he wasn't just a warrior—he was a **master of emotional intelligence.**

When he finally returned home to Ithaca after 20 years, he found that his wife was surrounded by suitors who had taken over his kingdom, believing him to be dead. He could have stormed in, sword blazing, and acted on raw rage.

But he didn't.

Instead, he disguised himself as a beggar and observed. He controlled his emotions, assessed the situation, and struck only when the time was right.

His patience and emotional mastery won him back his home, wife, and throne.

In today's world, strategy isn't just about business plans—it's emotional restraint in a heated meeting or choosing silence when anger tempts you to lash out.

Now, imagine if you applied this wisdom to your own life. What if, instead of reacting immediately to every emotional trigger, you **paused, assessed, and responded strategically?**

Be like Odysseus in your own life. Observe before reacting. Love and nurture yourself before making decisions. Serve yourself first—not in selfishness, but in self-mastery. The ability to control thoughts and emotions is your most extraordinary power. You are not your emotions; you are their master.

That's the power of emotional control.

Feelings Are the Expressions of Our Beauty

Feelings are not a weakness—they are what make us human.

The ability to feel deeply is a treasure: joy that lifts a room, sadness that deepens our empathy, anger that awakens our boundaries, love that breaks us open. These feelings are your beauty.

When you meet someone who cannot cry, smile, or get angry, you're not meeting a strong person—you're meeting someone burdened by unresolved emotions they've buried deep inside. The beauty of feelings lies in their variety. The ability to laugh at a simple joke, tear up at a song, or feel warmth from a stranger's kindness—*this* is what makes life worth living.

When expressed openly and authentically, feelings have the power to change the world.

The problem isn't emotions—it's the way we communicate them.

Mastering Your Feelings Makes You Irresistible

Want to know the secret to true magnetism? It's not looks, money, or status.

It's emotional presence.

When you master your feelings and express them genuinely and healthily, people are drawn to you. They feel safe around you. They trust you. They want to be near you. So many people are emotionally lost; they don't know how to handle their feelings, let alone connect with someone else's.

When you can:

- *Speak about your emotions without shame*
- *Express joy fully*
- *Handle anger without being destructive*
- *Listen deeply to others' emotions*

You become irresistible. You become someone people remember—not because of what you said or did, but because of how you made them feel. When you master your feelings, your presence lingers long after your words are gone.

Maya Angelou once said:

"People will forget what you said and did, but never forget how you made them feel."

Master your emotions, and you master your life.

The Decision to Master Yourself

Think back to a time when your emotions ran the show. Maybe you said something in anger that you later regretted. Perhaps you let fear stop you from pursuing something meaningful. Maybe you allowed self-doubt to talk you out of an opportunity meant for you.

Now, imagine how different your life would be if, in those moments, you had chosen emotional mastery.

What if you paused and responded with wisdom instead of reacting impulsively? What if you used emotions as signposts guiding you toward deeper self-awareness instead of letting them control you? What if, instead of believing every thought and feeling that arose, you questioned them and redirected your energy where it truly mattered?

This is your moment. You are no longer at the mercy of your emotions—you are in command.

Every time you practice awareness, shift your perspective, and choose calm over chaos, you take another step toward becoming the highest version of yourself.

And trust me—it looks good on you.

You Are Not Your Emotions—You Are Their Master.

Emotional mastery isn't about avoiding sadness, anger, or fear; it's about recognizing that these emotions are temporary and that you always have the power to choose your response. Master your emotions, and you master your life. The best part? You don't need anyone's permission to do this. Everything you need is already within you.

You are not at the mercy of your emotions. They are tools, not dictators. The more you learn to control them, the more creative, clear-minded, and successful you become.

Start by observing yourself.

The next time frustration arises, take a deep breath and ask:

- *Am I reacting, or am I choosing my response? What's the bigger picture?*

When anxiety creeps in, remind yourself:

- *Am I stuck in an old emotional script, or can I rewrite this moment? I have handled worse before. I will handle this, too.*

When self-doubt appears, ask yourself:

- *Am I letting emotions rule me, or am I using them to create something powerful? Would I talk this way to a friend? If not, why am I doing it to myself?*

Nothing controls you unless you hand it the reins.

Step into your power. Direct the inner stage. The next act is yours to write.

Now that you're mastering emotional control, the next step is identifying and fulfilling your core emotional needs. What truly drives you? What do you need to feel whole? In the next chapter, we dive deep into understanding your most fundamental desires—and how to meet them with power and clarity.

CHAPTER 7
You Are Not the Wound but the Healer

Who You Were This Morning Is Already Gone.

"I knew who I was this morning,
but I've changed several times since then."

— Lewis Carroll, *Alice in Wonderland*

Lewis knew. And now, so does science. Every day, every seven seconds, your cells regenerate. Your brain rewires. Your soul reaches forward—even when you feel stuck. So, let's ask the most daring question of this book so far:

Where is your trauma now?

Not yesterday. Not back in your childhood. Not on your ex's couch or in the middle of your worst moment. Right now. At this very moment. Is it a fact—or is it a story? Like believing you're unlovable because one person left you or thinking you're not capable because someone once told you so.

Trauma may have shaped us, but it doesn't have to dictate our destiny. That pain you carry? It's real, yes. But it's not your identity.

You are not your wounds. You are not your coping mechanisms. You are the one with the flashlight, not the cave. You choose which corners to illuminate—and which stories to rewrite in the light.

Let's stop sugarcoating: life hurts sometimes. But you were never meant to stay hurt. That's not why you're here. Let's find your way back to your heart—the compass, the charger, the quiet truth-teller you've always had.

You were not born to fail. That's a myth. You were born to grow, to try again, and to become someone this world needs.

You are not an accident. You are part of a precise, unrepeatable pattern—threaded perfectly into the tapestry of life.

You're here because this world can't do without you. That's not motivational fluff—it's physics. Remove one thread from the tapestry, and the whole design shifts. You're part of this pattern. You matter. Your unique value is irreplaceable.

Strength from the Heart

Let's talk about your heart—not the Instagram version, but the real one. That soft, electric drum inside your chest is not just there to feel pain. That's a misuse of its power.

Your heart is built for courage, not suffering. It is there to nurture you, to remind you of your softness *and* your fire, and to whisper,

"Keep going; I'm still beating for you."

So why don't we listen to it more? Because we've been taught to treat emotions like interruptions instead of **sacred messengers**. Your heart doesn't speak in essays or long, rational explanations. It speaks in pulses, in quick, instinctive reactions. In tears. In warmth. In chills.

And when it breaks? It's just stretching to let more truth in, not failing. Growing.

Stop Riding the Emotional Roller Coaster Without Reading the Safety Manual

Trauma makes everything feel urgent. It wants you to panic. But growth whispers,

"Pause. Observe. Study."

Here's your new mantra:

Study; don't spiral.

When emotions rise like a roller coaster, don't just hang on screaming.

Take notes. Get curious.

Study your reactions like a scientist. Study people. Study the world.

Do it

without judgment,
without commentary.
Just witness.

Watch how people hold their fear. Observe what makes them laugh. Notice how often they try to be right instead of kind.

There are no real failures—only edits. Rewrites. Staircases disguised as stumbles.

We inherited the idea of failure. But just because Grandma believed in it doesn't mean you have to.

Your Core Beliefs Are Not Obstacles— They're Rocket Fuel

Some of your beliefs were born in hard times. In loneliness. In rejection. In needing to survive. And that's okay. That doesn't make them shameful. That makes them **powerful**. They are your fingerprints. Your unique way of translating life.

And now, they are fuel.

When you say, "I want more," that's not greed. That's memory. The memory of your highest self echoes through time, saying: **You're meant for more**. You've heard that voice your whole life—it's not a fantasy. It's a *reminder*.

You're not reading this book by accident. You're here because a part of you already chose healing—even before you knew it.

So the question is no longer, "Why did this happen to me?"

The question is, "What am I meant to create because it did?"

You are not Your Trauma; You are the One Holding the Map

You are not your trauma—you're the storyteller who survived it and now rewrites the next chapter.

Here's a radical idea: your trauma is not the deepest part of you.

It's the *loudest*, maybe. But not the deepest.

The deepest part is the one reading this with curiosity. The one asking questions. The one ready to love again, trust again, dream again. The one who dares to say,

Maybe I'm stronger than I believed.

And if right now you feel stuck, like you're anchored to your trauma—talk. Share. Ask for help. Not because you're weak, but because **you're wise**. Carrying pain alone is not noble. It's unnecessary. Don't turn it into a behavior that wounds both yourself and those who love you.

Healing is not a solo performance. It's a symphony. Get your people.

Two Real People. Two Different Traumas. One Common Truth

Mateo grew up in a house where success was everything and emotions were a weakness. When he cried as a boy, his father would say, *"What's that going to solve?"* As an adult, he built companies that soared—until they didn't. His self-worth crashed with every financial dip. The trauma? A chronic emotional invalidation. The core need? *To feel safe in expressing vulnerability without punishment.* Mateo's real healing began when he stopped performing successfully and started practicing *being seen*—honestly, and tearfully.

Katerina survived a violent home. Her instinct was always to stay small, silent, and unnoticed. *"If they don't see me, they can't hurt me,"* she thought. She became the "good girl," the helper, the invisible rock. The trauma? Physical and emotional abuse. The core need? *To feel worthy of protection and visibility.* Her transformation started when she took up space—speaking in meetings, drawing boundaries, and even wearing bold colors. Her voice became her revolution.

Katerina learned that visibility is not vulnerability—it's power reclaimed.

The Truth About Trauma and Core Needs

Core emotional needs aren't luxury items. They are your emotional vitamins:

The need to be seen
The need to belong
The need to feel safe
The need to feel valued
The need to express truth
The need to be free

When trauma happens, these needs become interrupted, delayed, or repressed. But they never disappear. They become the silent architects of your behavior—until you become aware.

The key?

Don't try to erase your trauma. Understand it.

Ask:

What core need was unmet?
Where is that need showing up now—dressed as overachievement, avoidance, people-pleasing, or control?

This awareness doesn't just lead to healing; it leads to **freedom**.

The Roadmap: The Everyday Practice of Returning to You

Step 1: The 3-Minute Morning Check-In Before checking your phone, check yourself.

Ask:

What am I feeling today?
What do I need emotionally right now?
Can I give it to myself before I expect it from the world?

Even if the answer is "I don't know," you're already listening. That's the power.

Step 2: The "Is This Mine?"

Pause.

When you catch yourself reacting—snapping, hiding, over-explaining—stop.

Breathe.
Ask:

Is this reaction mine, or is it inherited?
What belief is running the show right now?

This uncovers the subconscious programming of society, family, and past pain.

Step 3: The Heart Strength Reminder

Say to yourself—out loud if you need to:

My heart is here not to punish me; it is here to nourish me.
I am not here to suffer; I am here to grow.
Even if I felt stuck yesterday, I'm allowed to change today.

This reassures your nervous system that it's safe to evolve.

Step 4: The Non-judgmental Study

From now on, observe yourself or others without judgment. Notice what people need, what they hide, and what they crave. Just observe—quietly and curiously, like a loving scientist. This will sharpen your perception and enhance your emotional intelligence.

Step 5: The Legacy Activation

At the end of your day, write this:

Today I showed up for my legacy by...

It could be small: *I drank water instead of skipping breakfast.*

It could be bold: *I said "no" for the first time.*

But it will remind you—*you are building something that will outlive your pain.*

The Future Is Already Whispering Your Name

In the distant future—and I mean truly distant—there may come a time when humans possess such emotional intelligence that empathy feels as natural as breathing. A time when theater serves not just as entertainment but as a sacred ritual of remembering who we are and where we've been.

In that future, we will realize:

Love is not a luxury. Peace is not a dream.

And the heart is not a battlefield.

It's a compass.

I call that future the irreducible Whole, where ethos, intelligence, and empathy coexist. But here's the beautiful secret:

- *You don't have to wait for the future to start living as if you belong in it.*
- *You are already becoming it.*
- *Every moment you choose truth over fear.*
- *Every time you study instead of judge.*
- *Every time you listen to your heart rather than your trauma.*
- *You are building a future where love leads.*

That is a legacy worth living for.

So here we are. You are not your traumas or the stories you once told yourself. You are the creator of your own experience. When you identify and meet your core emotional needs, life transforms from a battlefield into an open road of endless possibilities.

You've changed. Again. Since the first line of this chapter. Maybe not dramatically, but subtly. Quietly. And perhaps, something inside you just said:

I am not my pain. I am the one who chose to survive it. And now—I choose to live. Not just to survive, but to sing. Quietly at first. Then louder.

Good choice. Let's keep going.

The next chapter reveals the secrets to unlocking your inner genius. Once you align your emotional needs, your creativity and insight will skyrocket.

Are you ready to meet the most brilliant version of yourself?

CHAPTER 8

Unleashing Creativity and Vision

Creativity: The Driving Force of Evolution

Imagine if creativity wasn't confined to galleries or reserved for geniuses, but infused into how you communicate with your child, tackle a work challenge, or greet a stranger. What if it's not just about painting canvases, but about infusing every moment with purpose, insight, and presence?

Because here's the truth: your greatest masterpiece isn't hanging in a gallery. It's *you*—how you speak, love, lead, stumble, and rise. It's about thinking differently, solving problems, dreaming out loud, and daring to be seen. The power of your creativity shapes every aspect of your life, granting you the control to make it a work of art.

The world as we know it is built on creativity, which has been humanity's ultimate survival tool since the dawn of time. Our primal ancestors didn't just survive—they thrived. They crafted tools, created fire, shared stories around campfires, painted caves, beat drums, and embodied myth. The greatest minds—Einstein, Da Vinci, Tesla, Shakespeare—were not only intelligent; they were profoundly creative.

Your mind isn't merely absorbing the world—it's shaping it. Every belief, every choice is a brushstroke on your life's canvas. Are you painting with intention, or letting unconscious habits hold the brush?

The question is:

Are you creating consciously or unconsciously?

How many people do you know—accountants, lawyers, CEOs, plumbers, politicians—who've whispered, *"I wanted to be an actor,"* or *"I used to dance,"* or _"I still paint when no one's looking"? How many light up when they sing karaoke, tell stories, or craft something with their hands? That isn't nostalgia. **That's the soul trying to breathe. It's a universal truth that we are all born creators, imaginers, and storytellers, regardless of our professions or life paths.**
Creation is in our DNA. It's not a luxury—it's a vital life force.

It's like cutting off our oxygen when we silence that force and ignore the fire. We become numb, frozen—alive, perhaps, but barely living. Without expression, we are ghosts in our own lives.

Ignite your light. Set it free.

Reclaim the part of you that was never meant to be subdued. When you create—*truly create*—you rediscover yourself. You come back to life. This journey of self-discovery and personal growth is hopeful, leading you to a more fulfilling existence.

Creativity isn't a skill reserved for a select few—it's an innate force within all of us, a fundamental aspect of being human. This chapter explores how to tap into this infinite resource, break free from creative blocks, and reimagine your potential.

You Are the Creator

You're not just living in reality—you're shaping it.

Let's shake things up right now.

You've probably heard of *quantum physics* and thought, *"That's not for me. I'm not a scientist."* But what if, in *simple* terms, quantum physics is about the power of your thoughts, emotions, and everyday life?

You don't need a lab coat to grasp this.
You just need to be curious about *why your life feels the way it does.*

Because here's the truth:

You're not just observing reality. You're shaping it.

Your consciousness—thoughts, beliefs, emotions, and perceptions—is not some invisible fog floating in your head. It's a creative force. Think of your mind as a giant movie projector. Whatever plays inside—your fears, hopes, and mindset—gets projected outward onto the screen of your life. That's why two people can experience the same world entirely differently.

Have you ever had a day where everything went wrong? You spilled your coffee, missed your ride, and argued with someone you care about. It felt like the universe was against you. But it wasn't bad luck. It was a pattern. Your *inner world* shapes how you navigate the outer world. Now, here's the powerful part:

When you shift your inner world, your outer world starts to change.

That's not wishful thinking. That's quantum physics in action—the same principle that lets light behave as both particle and wave, now revealing your thoughts as energy with impact. And it's not just about particles and waves; it's about the power of your mind to shape your reality and create the life you desire.

The observer effect is a fundamental, tested principle showing that *observing* something changes its behavior. This means your attention, focus, and inner energy don't just remain inside; they *interact* with everything around you.

The Illusion of Reality—And How You Wake Up From It

Quantum physics offers a profound truth: reality isn't as solid as it seems. What we call "the real world" is built from energy and probability, shaped by our observation and perception. It is termed the illusion of reality—not because life is fake, but because it's *fluid*, malleable, and interactive.

Your consciousness is the paintbrush, and reality is the evolving canvas. Every thought, emotion, and choice adds color to the page.
Your psyche is the canvas.
And your reality? That's the painting you wake up in every day.

Once you understand this, everything changes.

You realize you're not trapped by circumstance; you're engaged in creation. You're not at the mercy of reality; you're in a relationship with it.

Why Are We Told Not to Use the Word "Quantum"?

Here's the strange part: even as quantum physics opens doors to deeper self-understanding, many scientists, academics, and skeptics *forbid* seekers and creatives from using the term.

Why?

For some, *quantum* is considered sacred territory—reserved for equations, particles, and peer-reviewed journals. They argue you can't discuss it unless you're wearing a lab coat.

But here's a question worth asking:

- Who owns knowledge?
- Who decides what tools belong to humanity and which ones are off-limits?

If science is truly the pursuit of truth—an effort to understand how the world works and what it means to be human—how can we claim that this one word, this one field that touches both matter and meaning, is "forbidden" to those seeking insight and healing?

And isn't the deeper question this:

What if quantum thinking is not just about physics—but about freedom itself, about the courage to seek truth wherever it leads?

The Mind Beyond the Brain

What exactly *is* the mind?

Is it merely the brain acting as a biological supercomputer? Or is it something more?

The truth is, the mind isn't limited to the physical brain; it extends beyond it. It's the space where consciousness resides. It's where thoughts are born, dreams take shape, creativity flows, and insight reveals itself. It's where you 'just know' something before it happens, feel a truth in your gut, or receive a flash of inspiration you didn't consciously think through.

Imagine you're an actor playing different roles in your life—friend, parent, entrepreneur, artist, student. Each role is like a costume you wear. But beneath them all is *you*—the director, the scriptwriter, the observer, and the creator.

You're not just reacting to life; you're shaping it.

Whether you realize it or not, every thought and action contributes to your unfolding story.

The big question is:

Are you writing the story you want to live?

The Archetypal Blueprint of Creativity

The ancient Greeks understood creativity as something beyond the individual. They perceived it as a connection to the divine—an alignment with the higher self.

In the center of the ancient theater stage was the *thymeli*, a sacred space where no actor could tread. It represented the pure psyche—the unfiltered truth, the core of human existence beyond social roles. It was the birthplace of creativity, where inspiration was not just an idea but a force of nature.

Like the *thymeli*, your creative essence is untouchable. It exists beyond the roles in your life, beyond your fears. It is the part of you that remains unchanged despite external circumstances. The more you align with it, the more effortlessly creativity flows through you.

Real-Life Stories: Creativity as a Guiding Force

My Creative Alchemy

My guiding force: I was never the student who excelled in math. I never completed a mathematics exercise in school. Chemistry? A mystery. But something inside me was always drawn to the philosophy of physics—the way it seeks to explain the universe, the unseen forces, and the intricate dance of energy and matter.

Creativity, for me, has never been confined to the arts. It is the vital force that propels me toward understanding who I truly am and why I'm here. It's not just something I *do*—it's how I *become*. It became the bridge between art and science. It wasn't about memorizing formulas but understanding the underlying patterns of existence.

When I immersed myself in the sciences, my creativity found its rhythm, its language. Suddenly, there was structure to the flow—reason behind the passion, meaning behind the expression. I understood why I am an artist. And in that union of heart and intellect, I became whole—again and again, every day.

That fusion became my secret power. I discovered a new way of thinking—beyond the conservative, black-and-white mindset we are taught. It allowed me to see connections where others saw chaos, to offer answers to questions most people never dare to ask—or don't even know exist. Somewhere along that path, I became something I never set out to be: a mentor, a guide, and a mirror for others. I never aimed for that. My only dream was to be an actor—because that's what my past self believed was the destination. But it was only the beginning.

Once I delved into my depths, into insight, awareness, and supraconscious truth, I discovered something far greater than a role. I discovered me—the one beyond the role, the one who had always been waiting to be remembered.

Vera Brandes – The Young Woman Who Healed Through Sound

Vera Brandes was a young German music producer who, at just 17 years old, organized the now-legendary 1975 *Köln Concert* with jazz pianist Keith Jarrett. But this wasn't just a story of artistic success—it marked the beginning of a personal journey where creativity became her salvation.

Later in life, after experiencing devastating personal losses and chronic illness, Vera was diagnosed with a life-threatening autoimmune disease. Doctors offered little hope, and traditional treatments failed. Instead of surrendering, she turned to the one thing that had always resonated with her on a soul level: music.

Drawing from her deep understanding of sound frequencies, neuroscience, and ancient music traditions, she began creating structured soundscapes—compositions designed not for entertainment but for healing. These weren't just songs; they were carefully tuned audio experiences aimed at affecting the nervous system and promoting deep healing. She experimented on herself, and something miraculous began to happen. Her body responded, and her symptoms started to ease. Over time, she healed.

Her creative journey led to the birth of *Sanoson*, a company developing sound therapies for hospitals and mental health centers worldwide.

Creativity didn't just help Vera survive—it awakened a new purpose. What began as a love for music transformed into the instrument of her rebirth, allowing her to serve thousands in their healing journeys.

Design Your Original Blueprint: Foundational Questions for Creative Awakening

Whether you realize it or not, you are constantly creating. Every thought, emotion, and choice is an act of creation.

You can choose how you create, perceive, and shape your reality. The key is to embrace your creative power without limits.

To harness your creativity fully, you must define your guiding principles for approaching life and creation.

Here's your blueprint. Ask yourself:

Purpose & Vision

- What is my ultimate vision in life?
- What creative pursuits bring me the most joy?
- How would my life change if I truly believed my thoughts shape my reality?
- How would my life change if I took ownership of my vision?

Obstacles & Risks

- How do I respond to failure?
- Where am I playing it safe, and where can I take creative risks?
- What recurring patterns in my life might reflect my inner state?
- What labels or roles do I wear that no longer feel aligned?

Expression & Alignment

- How do I align my creativity with my higher purpose?
- Where in my life do I feel most creative? What happens when I follow that energy?

- How would my life change if I took ownership of the "movie" I am projecting into the world?

Before you begin your seven-day journey, take time to explore these foundational questions. They are not tasks—they are doorways. Write your answers honestly, reflect on them compassionately, and redefine them as you evolve.

There is no rush. **You ARE the path**, even if your mind tries to convince you otherwise. Resistance is natural—the mind's way of protecting old patterns. But transformation requires presence, not pressure.

Sit with your answers until they feel authentic. You'll know when it's time. When your heart says, *"This is me,"* begin. That is the moment the journey truly starts.

Unlocking Creative Potential: Your 7-Day Journey to Reclaiming the Blueprint of You

This seven-day manual invites you to remember who you are beneath the roles, fears, and expectations. Each day builds upon the last, guiding you toward unlocking the original blueprint of your creative being.

Day 1 – Remembering: Who Am I Without the Noise?

Theme: *Socratic Self-Inquiry*

Begin by turning inward. Who are you beneath the roles, achievements, and expectations?

Ask yourself:

- *Who am I if no one is watching?*
- *What did I love before I was told what to love?*
- *What do I deeply long to express but haven't dared to?*

Practice: *Write stream-of-consciousness style for 20 minutes. Let your pen or fingers move without editing, and let the truth spill out.*

Shift: *You are not here to become something but to remember what you already are.*

Day 2 – Disrupting the Pattern: The Power of Unlearning

Theme: *Dismantling Fear-Based Thinking*

What stories keep you small? What beliefs are no longer yours?

Ask yourself:

- *What am I afraid will happen if I fully express myself?*
- *Whose voice do I hear when I doubt my power?*
- *What if failure wasn't the end but the initiation?*

Practice: *Write a letter to your fear. Let it speak. Then, write your response as your higher self.*

Shift: *Replace "What if I fail?" with "What if I soar?"*

Day 3 – Entering the Portal: The Sacred Unknown

Theme: *Stepping Into the Unknown*

Creativity thrives at the edge of chaos and mystery. It lives in the unknown.

Ask yourself:

- *Where am I holding back out of fear of the unknown?*
- *What would happen if I trusted the process more than the plan?*

Practice: *Do something unfamiliar today—paint, dance, improvise, take a new route home—and let discomfort guide you.*

Shift: *"I surrender to wonder."*

Day 4 – Dreaming Awake: Activate Through Visualization

Theme: *Meditation & Imagination*

Your mind doesn't know the difference between what you imagine and what is "real." Use this power wisely.

Ask yourself:

- *What does my fully expressed self look and feel like?*
- *If I were already creating from my highest self, what would I be doing right now?*

Practice: *Spend 10 minutes visualizing yourself creating freely—on stage, on the canvas, writing, building, leading. Feel it in your body. Then, journal what came up.*

Shift: *Imagination is the rehearsal for manifestation.*

Day 5 – The Flow State: Finding Your Sacred Current

Theme: *Engaging in Flow States*

Flow is where time disappears, and you become the process.

- Ask yourself:
- *What absorbs me so wholly I lose track of time?*
- *What am I doing when I feel most me?*

Practice: *Choose one such activity and give it at least 45 uninterrupted minutes today. Let go of the outcome. Just do it.*

Shift: *The more often you visit flow, the more natural creativity becomes.*

Day 6 – Embodiment: Creation Through Movement

Theme: *Moving Creation Through the Body*

Your body is your first instrument of creation. Before language, before thought—there was movement.

Ask yourself:

- *Where do I feel blocked in my body?*
- *What would expressing joy, grief, and freedom through movement feel like?*

Practice: *Put on music that stirs you. Let your body lead. No mirrors. No choreography. Just raw, embodied creation.*
Shift: *"My body remembers how to be free."*

Day 7 – Becoming the Creator: Living as Art

Theme: *Integration and Rebirth*

You are not separate from creativity—you *are* creativity. From this day on, your life *is* the canvas.

Ask yourself:

- *What kind of world am I here to create?*
- *How can I turn ordinary moments into sacred acts of expression?*

Practice: *Design a daily ritual that reminds you of your creative self—lighting a candle, doing a 5-minute free-write, sketching in the morning, or humming while you cook. Small acts. Big shift.*
Shift: *"I am not just a creator. I am Creation itself."*

This journey doesn't end here.

Creativity Is a Way of Being

Revisit these questions. Reignite the flame whenever the world tries to dim it.

Creativity isn't something you attain—it's something you remember. It's how your soul navigates the world.

To create isn't about learning; it's about reclaiming. You were born of stardust and wonder, meant not just to survive but to shape meaning with every breath. The canvas is yours. Begin again, now.

In the next chapter, we delve into the power of mastering fear—because nothing stifles creativity faster than fear. But once you conquer it, *everything* becomes possible.
Ready to step into your fearless, creative self?

CHAPTER 9
Fear of Death, Fear of Life

Dancing with Shadows: Unveiling Fear, Defying Death

Think back to a moment when fear gripped you so tightly it dictated your every move. Perhaps it was standing backstage with your heart pounding before you spoke, hovering over the "send" button on a message that could change everything, or lying awake at night replaying every mistake as if the future depended on it.

That is what fear feels like—always nearby, always shaping your choices.

Fear is like a shadow: silent, constant, trailing behind you, growing larger when your inner light dims. But here's the secret: shadows only exist when something blocks the light. When you turn inward, shining the lamp of awareness, the shadow dissolves. In the fullness of your presence, fear has nowhere to hide.

Recall when fear gripped you so tightly that it made your choices for you? Perhaps it was the fear of failure that locked your dream away, the fear of rejection that silenced your truth, or the fear of the unknown that froze you in a moment that asked for courage. These fears may seem different on the surface but are branches of the same root.

At the core of every fear—be it embarrassment, abandonment, poverty, or loneliness—lies a single, primal terror: **the fear of death**.

Consider the sting of embarrassment: your cheeks flush, your chest tightens, and in that instant, it feels as if you've been cast out of belonging. Beneath the surface, the body reacts as though rejection were life-threatening—as if the tribe had turned its back and left you alone on the savannah.

Or think about financial fear. Losing a job, a home, or stability doesn't just trigger worries about bills; it awakens something deeper. The subconscious equates survival with security, so when money disappears, the nervous system interprets it as starvation, danger, even extinction.

These modern fears may appear as minor crises of image or circumstance, but at their root, they awaken the oldest fear of all: the fear that our existence could end, that we could vanish, unloved or unseen.

Not merely physical death, but the fear of ceasing to exist in someone's heart, the fear of being forgotten, of being insignificant, of living without purpose. This fear hides deep in the subconscious, quietly scripting the narrative of our lives.

But what if death—as we've come to fear it—is an illusion?

In this context, *illusion* means a belief or perception that appears real but is based on limited awareness. It's like mistaking a shadow for a monster. When we expand our consciousness and see ourselves beyond the body, the ego, and the surface, we discover a self that is not bound by time, loss, or death.

We humans are curious creatures. We carry this suitcase of memories—some cherished, some cringe-worthy—and call it "me." But here's the twist: memory, while helpful for recalling passwords and past heartbreaks, is not your true self. We confuse memory with identity. And because memory fades, death feels like deletion—but who you are is more than what you remember.

These concepts may be challenging for some to accept. I know they might frustrate you, even make you angry. That's okay. That's your ego speaking—the part of you deeply invested in your story, attachments, and losses. You might think, *"But I've lost people I loved. I've felt the pain of death. I fear the moment I have to face it again."* And I hear you. I've felt it too.

But what if the pain you feel isn't proof of the finality of death but of love that never dies? What if the end we dread is simply a shift, a doorway, a return? What if your true self—and theirs—cannot be touched by death because it was never born and can never die? Then fear becomes not a guide but a ghost—a shadow of misunderstanding.

Shine the light. See the whole picture. Watch fear—and the illusion of death—disappear into the brightness of your truth.

Understanding Fear of Death to Transcend It

To achieve **freedom and self-realization**, you must confront your fears—not flee from them. Confronting fear is not a sign of weakness but a display of strength and courage. Fear is the **body's defense mechanism**, an evolutionary trait that keeps us alive. But while fear was valid when we lived in caves and dodged saber-toothed tigers, today, it mostly keeps us small, caged, and afraid of taking risks that would lead us to expansion.

Fear of death is not the enemy. **It is a signpost telling** you where you need to go. The bigger the fear, the more critical the journey. Fear is not a hindrance but a guide, leading you toward self-realization and growth.

I'll repeat it because repetition is how new truths take root in the mind and heart.

Our ancient wiring doesn't distinguish between ego death and physical threat—the fear feels real either way.

Each fear mirrors a kind of death—the death of ego, connection, or identity.

Let's break it down:

Fear of Failure → The Death of the Ego (a.k.a. "Who will I be if I'm not impressive?")

Let's be honest—when you fear failure, you're not just scared of messing up a project or flopping a big idea. You're afraid of watching your beautifully curated, Instagram-filtered self-image crumble. That version of you that always knows what to say, gets the job done, and never sweats? Yes, that one.

Failure doesn't just threaten your to-do list—it threatens your entire sense of worth.

Why? Because your ego, that needy inner diva, thrives on applause and control. When failure walks in uninvited, the ego gasps, clutches its pearls, and faints dramatically. It feels like death... because, in a way, it *is*—the death of a persona you once depended on.

But don't worry, the real you is backstage, rolling its eyes.

Fear of Rejection → The Death of Social Belonging (a.k.a. "Please like me, I need to live")

Rejection doesn't just sting—it activates your inner caveman. Back in the day, if your tribe kicked you out, you were bear food. So even today, when someone ghosts you, doesn't invite you, or gives you *that* look, your nervous system thinks it's about to be eaten alive. Your brain screams, "We're not safe! Join the group chat or perish!"

The fear of rejection is the fear of emotional exile—of feeling unseen, unworthy, and disconnected. So we conform, shrink, overshare, or say yes when we want to scream no to stay inside the imaginary safety circle.

The real tribe shows up when you stop performing.

Fear of Change → The Death of Your Current Identity (a.k.a. "Who even am I without my routines?")

Change is terrifying because it demands a funeral... for your current identity. Yep, that comforting, predictable version of you who knows exactly how to function in *this* life?

Change says:

"Thanks for everything, but your shift's over."

And your ego? It panics.

"Wait, no! I had a five-year plan and a favorite mug!"

But transformation doesn't care about mugs. It rips the old labels off and invites you into the unknown, where the future you waits in sweatpants, slightly wiser and freer. Like in nature, something must die for something new to grow.

Yes, your comfort zone may rest in peace—but your soul? It's just getting started.

Understanding These Fears as Invitations to Growth

Every one of these fears signals an opportunity for expansion.

The death of the ego allows a more authentic self to emerge.
The death of belonging to one group opens the door to deeper, more genuine connections elsewhere.
The death of an old identity allows for the birth of a wiser, stronger you.

But what if life and death are merely two sides of the same coin, like waking and sleeping?

You are not just your physical body.
You are eternal consciousness having a temporary physical experience.

When you realize this, the fear of death dissolves because nothing can truly destroy you.

The challenge is to stop resisting these deaths and start seeing them as passages to something greater. Instead of clinging to the familiar, ask yourself:

What is waiting to be born in me?

Cosmic Being, Now Accepting Gravity: A Tale of Spiritual Jet Lag

Why would a soul, infinite and boundless, choose to descend into the limitations of a human body? Many spiritual traditions suggest that life is a school, an experience designed for growth. The body and the material world provide the perfect **contrast and resistance** needed for evolution.

Physicality as a Teacher

Welcome to Earth School — No Refunds!

In the formless realms of pure consciousness, everything is smooth sailing. No struggle, no drama, no Wi-Fi passwords—just being.

But here's the kicker: To *understand* love, courage, forgiveness, and wisdom, your soul has to get its hands a little dirty. By "dirty," we mean experiencing fear, betrayal, heartbreak, and that one time you trusted the wrong person with your favorite mug.

We grow in contrast. Like a pearl formed through irritation, we evolve through tension.
Physical life is like the ultimate spiritual boot camp—minus the six-pack abs.

Time as a Lens

Why Does Everything Take Longer Than You Want It To?

In the eternal, time doesn't exist; it's all "now." But here in human land, we move moment by moment, like cosmic toddlers learning to walk.

Time helps us grow—one awkward decision and one deeply questionable haircut at a time. Every choice either expands our consciousness or makes us say, "Welp, I won't do *that* again."

It's slow, yes, but also profoundly personal. Enlightenment is, it turns out, a very patient process.

Duality as a Mirror

Without contrast, we wouldn't recognize our light. Duality gives us the mirror we need to remember our true nature.

Here's the paradox: We learn about light by encountering the dark. The temporary illusion of separation from the Divine—whether you call it Source, the Universe, or just "That Feeling When You Know You're More"—creates the perfect mirror for remembering who we really are. It's like cosmic hide-and-seek: the soul forgets so it can revel in the joy of remembering. (And occasionally scream-cry into a pillow along the way.)

Yes—being human is messy, weird, painful, hilarious, and wildly beautiful. But more than anything, it's a journey of remembering.

Remember that we are love. That we are infinite.

And somehow, all the nonsense and magic we experience is shaping us into exactly who we came here to be.

Returning to the Infinite: What Happens After Death?

If life is just one chapter in the soul's journey, then death is not an end but a return. Imagine leaving for a great adventure and then coming home to share your stories. That is what the soul does.

Death as a Transition, Not an End

It's Not Goodbye, It's Just a Costume Change!

Death gets a bad rap, but it's the soul's dramatic way of exiting the stage and heading backstage for a wardrobe change.

It's a shift, not a shutdown, like a caterpillar turning into a butterfly—except with slightly less cocoon and more mystery.

The physical body is left behind, like an old sweater you've outgrown, while the soul stretches back into its whole, expansive self. No, there's no pop-up window saying, "You've reached the end of your trial," just a smooth transition into something vaster.

Death as an ending, separation, and oblivion are illusions. Understanding this truth can bring a sense of relief and freedom, dissolving the fear that feeds on them.

The Life Review

This Is Your Soul's Highlight Reel… and Bloopers!

According to many spiritual traditions—and quite a few folks who've had near-death experiences and lived to blog about it—the soul goes through a life review.

But don't worry; it's not some terrifying cosmic court trial. It's more like watching your movie, with popcorn optional, where you feel what others feel because of your actions. It's not about guilt-tripping you; it's about understanding.

The key questions?

How much did you love? How much did you grow? Did you follow your soul's GPS or just keep recalculating?

Reintegration into the Infinite

Returning to the Group Chat of the Universe!

Once the body is off the to-do list, the soul flows back into the infinite—like logging out of the simulation and realizing you were connected to the Wi-Fi of all existence the whole time.

According to many traditions, this is where we experience oneness, healing, and divine "Oh, *that's* why that happened" clarity.

Some souls choose to come *back! Earth is weirdly irresistible!* While others continue evolving in realms without traffic, taxes, or tangled headphone cords.

The Liberation of This Perspective

Understanding life from the perspective of the soul changes everything. When you realize you are more than this body, more than this moment, the fears that once felt paralyzing begin to dissolve. What once looked like barriers are revealed as invitations to live more fully.

- **Fear of Failure Disappears.** If life is simply a classroom, then failure is not a punishment but a lesson. Every setback becomes material for growth. Think of the job interview you didn't get, only to discover it freed you for the opportunity that truly aligned with your gifts. Failure becomes not an ending but a redirection toward authenticity.

- **Love Becomes Fearless.** If you are eternal, then love is never truly lost. We carry every bond beyond this life. Even heartbreak becomes sacred proof of our capacity to connect. Remember the relationship that ended painfully yet left you wiser, more open, and more capable of loving deeply the next time. Love hurts, yes, but love never dies.

- **Risk-Taking Becomes Natural.** When you understand this life is one chapter in a much larger story, you stop holding back. You finally pitch the business idea, write the book, or speak your truth because you realize that regret weighs more heavily than rejection. The soul came here to expand—and risk is simply the doorway to that expansion.

- **Death Loses Its Power.** The fear of death, which governs so many human actions, begins to dissolve. You see that life is not a line ending in darkness, but a circle of becoming, where nothing is truly lost—only transformed.

In this view, **nothing is ever truly** *lost—only* **transformed,** *like ice becoming water, becoming vapor. And in realizing this, you become free.*

Free to live boldly, love fiercely, and embrace every moment as part of the sacred unfolding of your soul's eternal journey.

From Panic to Power: Fear-Facing Strategies for Highly Evolved and Slightly Nervous Humans

- **Acknowledge It.** Stop running from the fear of death. Look it in the eyes. Name it. When you acknowledge it, it starts to lose its grip.

  Example: Imagine you're terrified of public speaking. Instead of pretending you're fine, you admit, "Yes, I'm scared." That honesty deflates the monster in the dark and makes it something you can work with.

- **Shift Your Perspective.** Instead of seeing death as an enemy, view it as a mentor. Your fear reveals where growth is waiting.

  Example: A breakup can feel like the death of your world. But if you shift your perspective, it becomes a teacher—showing you where you lost yourself and where you now have the chance to reclaim your power.

- **Expose Yourself Gradually.** When faced with death, your fear shrinks, and your soul rises fearlessly. If you fear public speaking, start by speaking in small groups. If you fear rejection, practice expressing your opinions without attachment to approval. Each small step dissolves the illusion of danger and awakens the courage already within you.

Example: Afraid of heights? You don't need to skydive tomorrow. Start by standing on a balcony, then climb a hill, then take that hike with the cliff view. Step by step, your courage builds.

- **Rewire the Brain with Gratitude.** Gratitude is the ultimate weapon against the fear of death. The moment you are grateful for life, your fear weakens. The more you appreciate the present, the less you fear what's ahead

  Example: Each night, write down three things you're grateful for—even small ones like a smile from a stranger or the taste of your morning coffee. Over time, gratitude shifts your focus from what you might lose to what you already have.

The Existential Self Exercise

From the dawn of time, humans have sought answers to existential questions. We need explanations for what we perceive and experience. But what if the answer is not outside of us but within?

Try this exercise for a few weeks. Approach it gently, with curiosity rather than pressure.

1. **Stand before the mirror.** Each morning, give yourself 20 quiet minutes. Let this be sacred time.
2. **Observe your face.** Notice its lines, colors, and imperfections. Resist the urge to judge—simply witness.

3. **Meet your own eyes.** Gaze deeply into your right eye (or the left if you are looking at another). Go beyond the surface, into the soul behind the body.

4. **Stay with the shift.** At first, fear or discomfort may arise—this is the ego resisting. Do not run. Breathe and remain.

5. **Recognize the deeper self.** Over time, you will sense the presence beyond name, age, or form—the existential self, vast and eternal.

6. **Receive the reflection.** Let the mirror show you what you have always been: that every judgment is of yourself, and every act of love is also self-love.

At first, it may feel strange, even unsettling. But stay with it. With practice, fear dissolves. What remains is self-awareness, truth, and love. Fear cannot survive in the presence of light.

Stories of Fear-Based Paralysis and Triumph

Viktor Frankl — Meaning as the Antidote to Fear

The most profound antidote to the fear of death is meaning. When you understand why you live, death loses its power to paralyze you. This truth is evident in the life of Viktor Frankl.

Imprisoned in four Nazi concentration camps, including Auschwitz, Frankl confronted death daily. He lost his parents, brother, and pregnant wife. At any moment, he could have been sent to the gas chamber. Yet instead of succumbing to despair, he discovered something radical: even in the face of unimaginable suffering, one thing remained untouched — the freedom to choose meaning.

He observed that those who had a reason to live — who viewed their existence as purposeful — were more likely to survive. Frankl envisioned himself lecturing after the war, teaching others that life could be meaningful even in the darkest conditions. That vision provided him the strength to endure.

Frankl later wrote: *"Everything can be taken from a man but one thing: the last of the human freedoms — to choose one's attitude in any given set of circumstances, to choose one's way."*

His lesson is clear: fear of death loses its grip when life has meaning. By shifting the question from *"What can I expect from life?"* to *"What does life expect from me?"*, Frankl transcended fear and transformed his suffering into service.

Frankl didn't just survive; he lived with dignity, presence, and compassion, turning his personal trial into a beacon of wisdom for millions.

Antoine Leiris — Choosing Love Over Fear

On November 13, 2015, during the Paris terrorist attacks, Antoine Leiris lost his wife, Hélène, at the Bataclan concert hall. She was the mother of their 17-month-old son, Melvil. In a moment when grief and rage could have consumed him, Antoine made a radical, fearless choice: he refused to hate.

Just days later, he wrote an open letter to the terrorists that resonated worldwide: *"You will not have my hatred."*

He asserted that they had failed. He would not allow their violence to define him or poison his son's future. He chose to continue living, loving, and raising his child in light — not in fear. In that decision, he claimed his freedom.

His words did not deny his grief. He acknowledged his devastation, heartbreak, and pain. But he refused to let fear, anger, or hatred shape his next chapter. Instead, he chose presence. He chose love.

Here lies the lesson: when love leads, fear dissolves. Leiris demonstrates that even in the face of death, the greatest power we hold is the ability to decide how we will live. His story reminds us that love is not a fragile sentiment — it is the force strong enough to dismantle fear itself.

A Life Without the Fear of Death Awaits

Your fear of death is an invitation to growth. It is not meant to stop you but to challenge you. When confronted, it transforms into power. Your soul rises, fearless.

- *Do you fear failure? That's where your most significant success awaits.*
- *Do you fear rejection? That's where your most profound connections are born.*
- *Do you fear being seen? That's where your light is meant to shine.*
- *Do you fear being loved? That's where your deepest healing begins.*
- *Do you fear to love? That's where your true power awakens.*
- *Do you fear death? That's where your eternal self begins to live.*

Fear of death is merely a threshold. Step through it.

Imagine waking up every day unapologetically yourself— free to love, create, and pursue your destiny without hesitation.

A power awaits you—a savior for all—not outside, but within. You'll find it in the next chapter. It has been there all along — now you're ready to meet it.

Let's go there.

Together.

Where Do You Hold Your Power?

Now, I call this chapter *X*.

What sets this chapter apart is not just the words or tone but the unique perspective that emerged during the intense process of writing and editing this book.

A quiet pause.

A truth I couldn't overlook.

Now, I want to share it with you.

Amidst the plethora of motivational books, personal development courses, and life-changing workshops, there's a single, indispensable prerequisite that unlocks the door to personal growth: authenticity.

What is that thing?

It's this:

Being authentic.

Authenticity. Not polished. Not performative. Not perfect. But something unmistakably real — your soulprint, like a fingerprint that only you can leave on the world.

The kind of truth *"opposed to imitation"* is genuine, not an imitation, not a replica, no persona, no agenda, but something that comes directly from you, unmistakably real and unrepeatable. That doesn't belong to anyone else. It comes from only you, like your fingerprint.

No other human is on this planet with your exact print and unique authenticity.

That's what authenticity is: a soulprint. Unduplicated. Undeniable. Uncompromising.

It is that **spark**, that **light**, that **magic** few people we meet truly carry — the kind that makes you stop and think, *"There's something about them I can't even put into words — something magnetic, grounding, luminous. You just* **feel** *them."*

Before we proceed with anything else in this book, I challenge you to meet yourself here before we talk about genius, impact, alignment, and freedom. Not the self you show to others. Not the one you think you need to be.

The *real* you.

Don't mind me if I seem a little harsh in this chapter.

I'm not here to comfort you. I'm here to speak to your core.

Because truth without honesty is empty, and honesty without courage is silent.

If I ask you to be accurate, I have to start by being honest with you. So, here it is.

The chapter on **Authenticity**

Are You Performing or Living?

You are an actor — not by profession, but by conditioning. That's the twist.

Example: "Like the overachiever who never asked if their success was their own dream or just someone else's approval game."

The difference between an actor on stage and an actor in life is this: stage actors *study* the role. They delve deep. They understand the motivations, the wounds, and the backstory of the persona they're bringing to life. They consciously study the role's wants, needs, and behaviors. But most people in the real world? They perform characters they never question. Roles they inherited. Scripts they didn't write. The tragedy? They believe it's who they are.

Let's cut the fluff: authenticity isn't a trend; it's a revolution, a powerful force that can transform your life.

It's not about burning sage, wearing flowy pants, or shouting, "I'm living my truth!" from a mountaintop (though hey, if that's your vibe, go for it).

It's about **being you**—entirely, unapologetically—and **doing the messy, daily work** to become more of you.

Authenticity isn't performance. It's alignment.

It's when your values, choices, and actions are in harmony.

It's when you don't just *say* you care — you act like it.

It's when your Instagram bio doesn't say "Empath. Dreamer. Giver." while your life says "Manipulator. Excuse-maker. Approval junkie."

Don't claim to be a good person of faith if deep down you believe others — people with different religions, cultures, or identities — don't deserve the same rights as you. That's not faith. That's fear wearing a holy hat.

Don't say you're a good parent if you refuse to work on your emotional wounds and then unload your unhealed baggage on your kids. That's not parenting — that's projection.

Don't claim to be a good partner if you suffocate your other half, expect them to make you whole, and resent them for growing in a direction you disapprove of. That's not love. That's emotional hostage-taking.

Don't say you're a good politician if the laws you pass protect power more than people. That's not leadership. That's control in a three-piece suit.

Don't claim to be a people-first CEO if your hiring practices only serve your bottom line and you can't see a human beyond their performance in a 20-minute interview. That's not care. That's capitalism with a customer service smile.

Don't claim to be thriving if your days feel hollow and you've never stopped to ask why.

Don't say you're a giver if every "act of kindness" is secretly a boomerang — given to get. That's not generosity. That's manipulation in a mask.

And don't say you're a decent person if you trash-talk your neighbor behind their back or judge people simply because they make you uncomfortable. That's not decency. That's disguised superiority.

You don't have to agree with everyone, but you should respect their humanity.

Let's get real. Again.

Authenticity demands courage.

Authenticity is not a path paved with ease but *with* honesty. It begins with a radical form of self-reflection, where you don't shy away when the mirror reflects your truth.

So, ask yourself: *Where do you hold the power?*

Not in how you look. Not in what you own.

Not in who likes your posts.

You hold the power in the space between thought and action. That moment when fear whispers, "Play it safe," and you respond, "Not today." That moment when fear says 'shrink', and instead, you step forward, like cracking a door to your own potential.

You think a fearful thought, and immediately your stomach drops, your chest tightens, and your day dims. It happens.

We all experience it. But here's the magic move: When your eyes open and fear tries to beat you to the punch tomorrow morning, *catch it*. **Take the chance. Choose differently.**

Free will isn't a theory — it's your daily power move.

Don't let fear think for you.

Let your truth lead instead.

A life free from fear isn't some fantasy or philosophical abstraction. It's a way of being. It's the shift from **survival mode to soul mode**. When fear stops running the show, everything changes.

Authenticity becomes your baseline. No more shape-shifting to be liked. No more apologizing for your truth. No more trading peace for approval.

Like when you finally told your boss no without offering an explanation.

And the world didn't end.

Courage kicks in. Not because fear is gone — but because you're done letting it hold the mic.

When you choose truth over fear, something radical happens: Limitless potential?

That's not a motivational quote — it's what unfolds when you finally stop dragging the baggage of who you *think* you should be and start living as you are.

The best part?

Fearlessness is a skill.

You don't need to be born with it. You build it, breath by breath, choice by choice, honest moment by honest moment.

You breathe through discomfort. You pause instead of reacting.

You reframe fear as feedback, not a stop sign. Like a blinking light on your dashboard, not to halt you, but to get your attention.

And soon, you're no longer surviving your life — **you are creating it.**

Fully. Boldly. With a bright mind and an open heart.

Yes, you're going to mess up. You'll lose your way sometimes. That's part of it. But you'll keep returning to the truth. And that, dear reader, is the real flex.

Put simply?

Authenticity means your insides match your outsides.

- Your values match your choices.
- Your heart shows up in your life — not just in your journal.
- You become someone worth living as.
- Someone worth remembering.

So go on.

Get honest. Get loud. Get real.

And for the love of all things sacred and human — stop pretending. Perform authentic life acts. Share your truth, your light.

Your truth is not too much. It's the whole damn point.

The Freedom of Being True: Lessons from Mandela: A Masterclass in Authentic Leadership

If you ever wonder what authentic leadership looks like, remember this:

It's not polished. It's principled.

It's not loud. It's aligned.

And it's not always popular. But it *always* leaves the world better than it found it.

That's authenticity in power.

That's why Nelson Mandela's legacy didn't end with his presidency—it began there. He didn't just talk about freedom, dignity, and reconciliation—he lived them, suffered for them, and stayed aligned with them, even when it would've been more manageable—and far more convenient—to compromise.

Mandela spent twenty-seven years in prison, and when he finally walked free, the world expected rage, revenge, and retribution. Instead, he chose reconciliation over revenge, unity over bitterness, and principle over power.

He didn't say, "I forgive you" because it sounded noble.

He said it and meant it, because that was the only path aligned with his values. Unlike many leaders who chase political currency, Mandela refused to sell his people grand promises and then abandon them. He remained rooted in justice, compassion, and truth, even when it cost him comfort, risked misunderstanding, or made the path harder. Rather than bending to pressure to please one side or weaponizing his position to dominate and retaliate, he chose to heal, to bridge, and to lead from a place of grounded, hard-earned integrity.

Even when he became president, Mandela continued to embody humility and service. He wore the same sincerity whether speaking to world leaders or a child in a village. Perhaps that's the most powerful marker of authenticity: consistency, regardless of the spotlight. He never tried to be perfect. He was honest, disciplined, and devoted to a cause greater than himself.

Practical Steps to Living Authentically

How to Stop Being a Walking Mask and Start Being a Whole Human

Take Inauthenticity Out of the Driver's Seat

You've been performing — not as a stage actor but as a conditioned one. Taking on roles, scripts, and expectations you never questioned. Most people live like this — on autopilot, choosing what looks good, sounds smart, or keeps the peace. But authenticity doesn't do safe. It does truth.

Inauthentic decisions look like staying in a job you hate because your parents are proud, or posting filtered joy while falling apart inside.

Authentic decisions? They shock people. They shake things up. They sound like: "I'm not fine," "I want more," "I'm done pretending."

Start noticing where you bend to please, perform, or disappear. Then — lovingly, fiercely — choose truth instead.

Reframe Discomfort as a Sign of Alignment

Example: "Like when you told your partner you wanted more — terrified they'd leave. They didn't. And you finally felt seen."

Newsflash: authenticity isn't comfortable.

It's awkward. It's vulnerable.

When you stop pretending, you risk being seen and rejected. But you also open the door to being seen and *loved*. That's a big difference.

Feeling nervous about sharing the truth? That's not a red flag — that's a green light.

Afraid to tell someone how you feel? That means it *matters*.

Uncertain about stepping into a new version of yourself? Good. That's growth. That's life. That's *you* unfolding.

Authenticity doesn't guarantee comfort. It guarantees freedom.

Use the "What's the Worst That Could Happen if I Were Honest?" Trick

Your ego loves drama. It will convince you that telling the truth will ruin your job, image, relationships, and reputation.

But take a breath. Play it out.

You speak up at work. Worst case? They disagree. You survive. Best case? You gain respect.

You tell someone you're not okay. In the worst case, they get uncomfortable. In the best case, you connect deeper.

You walk away from what isn't aligned. Worst case? You feel uncertain for a while. Best case? You finally breathe.

Truth rarely burns your life down.

But inauthenticity slowly eats it from the inside out.

Make Authenticity Your North Star, Not Approval

Approval is weather — it changes daily. Alignment is your compass.

Authenticity is not about pleasing people. It's about being in integrity — with *yourself*.

Approval is fickle. One day, you're adored; the next, you're misunderstood.

Chasing approval is a losing game. But chasing alignment? That's where your peace lives.

So when the crowd says, "That's risky," and your heart says, "But it's real,"

Choose the heart—every time.

Talk to your inner people-pleaser like a well-meaning but outdated app: "Thanks for trying to keep me liked, but I'm going for aligned."

Embrace the Unknown

Stop Trying to Script Life Like a PowerPoint.

You can't be authentic and obsessed with control at the same time.

Because realness doesn't come with guarantees; it comes with presence.

You don't get to predict how your truth will land.

You don't get to package your transformation into a neat, digestible moment. You show up anyway.

Every meaningful moment in your life comes with uncertainty. Every person you've truly loved started as a stranger.

Every version of you that felt more you began in a moment of, "What if I just say it? What if I just go for it?"

Stop seeing the unknown as the enemy.

Start seeing it as where your authentic self is waiting to meet you.

Speak Like You Mean It: The Language of Authenticity

Create your authentic language.

Words are not just sounds — they are blueprints for reality.

Authenticity means aligning your heart with your mind; you do that by reframing every moment through your values.

Ask yourself constantly:

Does my language reflect who I am?

Does it uplift or diminish?

Does it hurt me? Others? The outcome I want?

Words matter. How you speak — to yourself, others, and the world—builds your truth or buries it.

Fear might still whisper, but authenticity speaks louder now. And it doesn't ask for permission.

Bottom line?

Living authentically isn't about eliminating fear.

It's about showing up *as yourself*— even when fear is tagging along.

It's about not claiming you're a giver when giving is how you manipulate.

Not saying you're kind when your thoughts about others drip with quiet judgment.

You should not call yourself decent when you are unkind to your neighbor, coworker, or a stranger who triggers you.

It's about **owning your contradictions** to work through them—not performing over them.

It's about **being the person you say you are**— especially when no one is watching.

Because a life of truth?

That's not just worth living.

That's the only kind worth remembering.

The Real Reason I'm Writing — A Closing That Opens

I will close this chapter with a little paradox — by opening something personal.

There's something I can't leave unwritten — something that shaped me as a human and fuels every word I write.

The next generations.

They are why I can't afford to pretend. What we normalize, they inherit.

A Lesson from My Father: A Tip for Parents *and Everyone Else, Too*

Fearless living doesn't just *start* in childhood — it *depends* on it.

If there's one thing my father did that shaped my soul, it was this: he didn't tell me who to be. He taught me how to be myself.

He never imposed when I stood at the edge of a big decision — the kind that makes your stomach knot. He didn't lecture, panic, or guilt me into the "right" choice. He calmly sat me down and said something like:

"If you go this way, here's what that might bring."

"If you choose the other path, this could happen instead."

"Now... which one sounds more like you? Which one helps you become more of who you're meant to be?"

He taught me to think with myself, not against myself.

To this day, that remains one of the greatest gifts I've ever received — not the avoidance of failure, but the inner compass to make authentic choices, not fear-based ones.

His words didn't build walls around me. They built wings.

My Transformation: My Choice to Be Real

Fearlessness isn't gifted — it's *built*.

Not in giant leaps, but in tiny, brutal, beautiful choices. I chose to live two lives in one. What does that mean?

It means I refused to live the life the world tried to assign me—the one rooted in fear, perfectionism, approval, and safety. Instead, I chose the life I knew in my bones was mine: one of truth, grit, mess, magic, and unrelenting authenticity.

There's a force in me — soul, spirit, fire — that won't let me play small, even when rejection knocks. Even when the bank account says, "Nice try." Even when fear whispers, "This is too much." I still choose the truth of me. I still decide to move.

Comfort isn't my goal — *becoming* is.

That is dynamic, authentic living: not waiting for permission, not letting your circumstances dictate your capacity. It's standing in the middle of chaos and saying, *"This is hard — but I'm still mine."*

Thank you, Dad!

Parents, listen up:

Your job isn't to mold your children into perfect people.

It's to guide them into real ones — people who know how to hear themselves, trust themselves, and walk their own path with courage.

Don't preach bravery while modeling fear.

Don't ask for truth from your child while hiding your own.

Don't perform "good parenting" while silently passing down unhealed patterns.

Be someone worth copying. That's the whole game.

Show them that choices carry power — not just consequences. That self-trust matters more than perfection. That honesty is a birthright, not a performance.

Because what we normalize, they inherit.

If we want a world of bold, kind, free people — it begins at the dinner table, the bedtime story, the ordinary Tuesday morning when we choose to be real instead of right.

Raise children who are not afraid of their voice.

One day, they'll become adults who are not afraid of their soul.

The world doesn't need more "perfect" people. It needs real ones.

And real people? They build themselves daily — one honest, terrifying, exhilarating, soul-aligned choice at a time.

So, as Chapter X ends, the real work begins. Building a life that doesn't just impress, but frees you.

The Genius Code

The Exhilaration of Discovering Your Genius

Imagine waking up one morning, stretching your arms, blinking at the ceiling, and suddenly realizing—

"Holy crap, I'm a genius!"

Not in the *'I-just-cured-cancer-while-baking-a-soufflé'* way (although, hey, aim high), but in a *profound, undeniable, wildly personal* way. A sort of genius that's been quietly living inside you all along—sipping tea, tapping its foot, wondering when you'll finally notice it.

But then that little voice pipes up—'Wait, me? Really?' And before you can savor it...

Let me stop you right there.

That. Is. The. Lie.

That's the programming. The conditioning. The outdated software you've been running since childhood.

Throughout history, society has treated genius like a competition—ranking, grading, and labeling it as if it belongs only to the elite few: the Einsteins, the da Vincis, the people with three PhDs and an asteroid named after them.

Genius, they say, is *rare*, it's *measurable*, and it's *other people*.

But here's the truth bomb:

Genius is not about IQ scores, standardized tests, or having your name etched on a plaque in a fancy hallway.

Genius is your unique way of seeing and shaping the world. It's the moment your hands move faster than your thoughts, or when you say the one thing in a room that shifts the whole energy. It's that spark you feel when you're creating something meaningful, solving a problem your way, or saying something that makes someone else stop in their tracks and go, "Wait—how did you think of that?"

It's when your heart, mind, and body suddenly align, and you feel *alive*.

That's genius. It's not mythical. It's not elite.

It's not far away. It's yours.

The real tragedy? Society has been grading us forever. From birth, we're sorted, ranked, praised, and punished based on systems that often have nothing to do with our true essence. We're trained to doubt ourselves, to shrink, and to believe that brilliance lives somewhere else, in someone else. This societal conditioning is the barrier that hinders us from recognizing our genius.

But look closer.

You've had those moments—those flashes when you did something and thought, *"Damn, that was kind of amazing,"* or someone turned to you and said, *"Dude, you're a genius."* You laughed it off, played it cool, but deep down? You knew they saw something. And you felt it, too.

Those aren't accidents. That's your inner genius saying, "Hi. I've been here all along."

We give meanings to words like *good and evil, smart and stupid, black and white*—but in the murky, magical in-between lies the truth:

Genius is the in-between.

It lives in the gray zones—where creativity dances with uncertainty, and the best ideas don't follow rules.

It's not about being "the best" or "the smartest" or reaching some mythic threshold like an IQ of 180 (which, for the record, Leta Hollingworth said only 1 in 2 million people reach—so stop comparing). It's about showing up as the most whole, most complementary, real version of you.

It's about unconditioning yourself.

Because the more conditioned you are, the more muted your genius becomes.

And the less conditioned you are—the freer, weirder, wilder, more *you* you allow yourself to be—the more that genius flows through everything you do.

This isn't spiritual fluff. It's real.

Think of the street artist whose mural healed a grieving community. That's not fluff—that's genius embodied.

You see it in people's eyes, in sparks of conversation, in moments of stillness, joy, or courage. You don't need a certificate to confirm it. You just need to remember.

So, here's the new understanding:

You are not *becoming* a genius.

You are *remembering* the genius you already are.

And once you unlock that—once you stop waiting for permission or validation—life will never be the same again.

You Are a Genius, Whether You Know It or Not

Each of us carries a powerful, untapped potential—an inner force that, if unleashed, transforms not only our own lives but the lives of those around us. The tragedy is that most people die with it still locked inside, their gifts never fully realized or shared. That loss isn't just personal; it's collective.

Why does it happen? Because we've been taught to believe brilliance comes in one narrow form. If you can't solve equations like Einstein or paint like Van Gogh, you're told you're ordinary. That's a lie.

Society trains us to overlook the extraordinary. Systems of power quietly decide who gets seen and who gets silenced. As a result, countless lives of originality pass unnoticed—not because they lacked greatness, but because the world never looked for it in the right places.

There have been moments in your life—just remember and revisit them. These moments are not ordinary; they are the seeds of your genius. You can reconnect with your innate potential by remembering and revisiting these moments.

Nothing is ordinary about genuinely caring for someone you love, about a grand gesture of kindness, or about sharing your smile with a friend. These moments are not given; they are created, and in their creation, they become precious.

Even in your darkest moments, when you feel no resistance left, there is still a spark—a quiet inner voice that whispers, "You know you are lying to yourself," or, more profoundly, "Do you know you are conditioned?" That voice echoes truth, reminding you that you were born to thrive, not to fail, to be happy, not to suffer.

Your genius isn't defined by societal values but by what makes **you** come alive. The world needs **your unique vision, voice, and understanding of life.**

How do we break the lock and set it free? Buckle up. We're about to find out. It's time to shatter societal norms and embrace your unique genius.

Recognizing the Seeds of Genius Within You

Think back to your childhood. **What sparked your curiosity?** What activities did you engage in purely for joy? What fascinated you so much that you lost track of time?

Like the girl who built birdhouses from cereal boxes to make robins feel safe in winter.

Perhaps you were the kid who disassembled radios just to see how they worked.

Maybe you had a knack for making people laugh with the perfect joke at the right moment.

Perhaps you could sense how people felt, even without words.

Or you might have been the one who created harmony amidst chaos.

These weren't mere hobbies—they were blueprints for who you were before the world taught you to doubt yourself.

Genius isn't something you "acquire" later in life. **It's something you've always possessed.** It's just been buried beneath years of societal conditioning, fear, and self-doubt.

The Genius Next Door: How Everyday Brilliance Quietly Changes the World

The Janitor Who Redesigned Hospital Safety

In a small-town hospital, a janitor named Samuel noticed patterns others overlooked. Each night, as the halls emptied, he walked them like a guardian, spotting smudges and unseen dangers.

He observed that infections spread not through surgeries but through seemingly small things like poorly cleaned door handles and neglected corners.

One day, he approached a nurse with a new cleaning routine—an innovative path through rooms, a timing system, and a color-coded method for sanitizing equipment. The hospital trialed his system, and infection rates dropped by 37% within months.

No one had solicited his input. He wasn't in a leadership position. But his mind made connections that others missed. His brilliance wasn't loud—it was *effective*. Patients improved. Nurses felt safer. And a humble janitor proved that genius isn't about your title; it's about how you *see* and *care*.

The Grandmother Who Invented a Communication Game

Maria, a grandmother in Athens, noticed her grandson with autism struggled to express himself. Rather than resorting to traditional speech therapy, she created a playful card game using colors, sounds, and facial expressions.

Soon, her grandson began connecting, smiling, and engaging. Other parents heard about it and wanted to try it. That simple game spread among families and therapists, becoming a local phenomenon—helping dozens of children feel understood for the first time.

Maria wasn't a trained psychologist and didn't publish a paper. But her genius lay in her deep empathy and creativity. She *listened* differently, and in doing so, she changed lives.

The Young Girl Who Reimagined Lunchtime

In a crowded public school cafeteria, 9-year-old Amina noticed something that most kids missed: some classmates rushed through lunch or pretended they weren't hungry. They joked and made excuses, but Amina *felt* something was off.

Instead of ignoring it, she began bringing extra snacks in her backpack—fruits, homemade sandwiches, and little notes with hearts and encouragement. She handed them out discreetly, never making a fuss.

One day, a teacher noticed. Instead of scolding her for "sharing food," the teacher asked Amina why she was doing it. Amina replied, "I think they're hungry and want them to feel okay." That conversation sparked a small school initiative where students could "donate" snacks anonymously to anyone in need. Within a month, no child in that school had to pretend they weren't hungry anymore.

Amina didn't write a proposal. She didn't wait for permission. She simply recognized a need, empathized with others, and responded with heart and creativity. That's genius.

Not measured by IQ, but by compassion and courage in action.

These are the kinds of genius society often overlooks—because it wears no medals, speaks in whispers, and changes the world from the inside out.

Techniques for Nurturing and Maximizing Your Potential

Permit Yourself to Be a Genius

Seriously. Do it. Right now. Out loud if you have to:

"I give myself permission to be a freaking genius."

For too long, people have been led to believe that embracing their genius is "arrogant." It's not. The real crime is **denying your gift** to the world.

Get Obsessed with Your Fascination

Geniuses aren't distracted by *everything*. They find what **lights them up** and go *deep*. They let curiosity consume them. They follow their instincts and dive into their work, **not for money or fame, but because they can't NOT do it.**

Like the woman who started making candles during quarantine and now runs a shop that funds community programs.

What fascinates you? Follow it. Explore it. **Let it become your playground.**

Create More Than You Consume

Most people drown in information but starve for creation.

Stop waiting. Start doing.

- Write the book.
- Start the business.
- Paint the masterpiece.
- Build the invention.
- Teach the class.

Stop waiting for permission. **No one is coming to anoint you. You must anoint yourself.**

Embrace the "Mad Scientist" Mentality

Geniuses don't play it safe. They experiment, make a mess, fail spectacularly, **and get back up.**

- Einstein was labeled "slow" in school. He changed physics forever.
- Oprah was fired from her first TV job but became one of the most influential voices in media.
- Colonel Sanders (the KFC guy) faced rejection 1,009 times before someone accepted his fried chicken recipe. One. Thousand. Nine. Times.

The lesson?

Genius isn't about being "perfect." It's about being relentless.

Society Said No, You Say Watch Me

Society Wants You to Play Small—Ignore It

The system isn't designed to support geniuses. It's built to create obedient workers who follow the rules.

Genius questions those rules. Genius challenges the status quo.

Genius refuses to accept mediocrity as normal.

You weren't meant to "fit in."

You are meant to stand out.

Get Comfortable Being Uncomfortable

Most people avoid discomfort. Geniuses **lean into it**.

Embrace uncertainty.

Welcome failure.

Seek challenges because that's where growth occurs.

The moment you stop running from discomfort is the moment you set your genius free.

Finally, Let Go of the "I'm Not Ready" Excuse

Newsflash:

No one is ever fully ready. The best way to become a genius is to start before you feel prepared.

Like the teen who launched a podcast from her bedroom— she now interviews CEOs.

Genius is built in the doing.

Genius Is Not a Gift—It's a Choice

Genius isn't some mystical gift handed out like a golden ticket at birth. It's a choice. A fire. A way of showing up in the world with your whole, unfiltered self. It's about recognizing the brilliance inside you, nurturing your curiosity as if it's sacred, and pursuing what ignites you with wild, unapologetic energy. It's about refusing to shrink into mediocrity simply because the world fears too much shine.

The truth?

The world doesn't just want your genius—it needs it.

Think about the moment you realized there's more to you than you've been led to believe. That there is **something inside you waiting to be unleashed.**

That moment was real. And it's time to act on it.

So stop waiting. Embrace your genius. Set it free. Burn bright. Be loud. Be you.

Now that you've unlocked your genius, it's time to live dynamically. Step into a life of passion, energy, and unstoppable momentum.

In the next chapter, we explore what it means to live at full capacity—where life stops happening to you and starts happening **as** you.

Now go light up the world—with everything you are.

CHAPTER 11

The Ultimate Quest for Dynamic Living

Remembering Dýnami: The Power You Forgot You Spoke

To reconnect with who we are and what we're truly capable of, we must journey back—not through time, but to our origins. We need to revisit the roots that still whisper through our everyday lives, even if we no longer hear them.

And here's the delightful twist:

You already speak Greek.

Not fluently or consciously, but in the architecture of your thoughts and the hidden scaffolding of your language, Greek supports the meanings you use daily.

Ever said 'photograph'? That's Greek for 'light-writing.' You're more ancient than you thought.

Consider the word dýnami. It's part of your everyday vocabulary, sounding firm and alive, like the hum of electricity before a thunderstorm.

Dýnami, derived from the ancient Greek verb *dýnamai*, meaning 'to be able', represents more than mere ability. It embodies energy, potential, inner strength, and the right to act. This concept transcends mere capability, empowering you with the raw materials for creation, transformation, and choice. Essentially, it's your inner power—the force that drives you to act and create in your life.

To possess *dýnami* is not just to be capable, but to be *empowered, to hold within you the raw materials for creation, transformation, and choice.*

It's the seed and the spark—the permission slip you don't need to ask for, the freedom to say, "I can," "I may," "I have the power (dýnami) to."

It's saying:

"I can." "I may."

"I have the power (dýnami) to."

When we talk about living dynamically, we're not adding something foreign to ourselves—we're reclaiming something ancient and beautifully familiar.

We're awakening the dýnami that was always there, waiting to be seen, spoken, and lived.

Life as an Expedition, With Coffee, Curiosity, and a Dash of Chaos

Imagine waking up every morning—not with a groan, a snooze button slap, or a silent prayer for five more minutes—but with the quiet thrill of an explorer about to embark on a once-in-a-lifetime expedition. Your bed? That's base camp. Your slippers? Hiking boots. Your to-do list? A treasure map. Does it sound like a fantasy? Maybe. But the truth is: this is how life *could* feel.

Sure, the dragons might be spreadsheets, and the treasure a quiet moment of peace—but that doesn't make the quest any less real.

Life *is* an expedition. An unpredictable, messy, hilarious, heart-expanding journey filled with dragons (some are emails), treasures (some are conversations), and magical portals (some look like traffic lights).

But here's the twist: most people aren't living like explorers.

They're living like pre-programmed tour guides on a loop. Wake up, repeat yesterday, try not to spill coffee, avoid existential crises, scroll, sleep, repeat. That's *routine*—and routine isn't the enemy. It keeps your teeth brushed and your cat fed.

However, routine is not the same as living an ordinary life. Living an ordinary life means going through the motions without much thought or intention. On the other hand, routine keeps your cat fed, but dynamic living nourishes your spirit. One is maintenance; the other is meaning.

Every day, you have the power to choose your path. It's *not just* about grand gestures, but the small, intentional decisions that shape *your life*. It starts with your first thought in the morning. That one little spark that asks,

"What could I discover today?"

And that's the secret. You don't need fireworks daily to create a pleasurable, meaningful life. You don't need to climb a mountain, launch a business, or write a book (although, sure, go for it). What you *do* need is a spark. A moment of thoughtfulness. A decision to *move forward*, however small, with intention. This could be as simple as pausing to admire the morning light, texting someone you love, choosing tea instead of stress, or allowing yourself to truly feel your thoughts.

Dynamic living isn't about being dramatic—it's about being deliberate.

It's understanding that your thoughts and feelings contribute to your identity, no matter how small they seem.

They shape your inner world. And when you go to bed at night, whether you crushed your to-do list or cried over your fourth existential meme of the day, you can still say:

"Thank you for adding wonder to my life today."

Because every day is here to serve you, not the other way around.

And here's something vital:

No one has the right to judge your life path. It's not a race; it's a constellation, and only you can read the stars.

Your expedition doesn't have to resemble anyone else's. Because it's not the path that defines your power—it's the intention behind each step. You may be one of those wonderful people for whom dynamic living means a peaceful rhythm—performing simple tasks with deep presence. Or you may thrive on movement, vision, and big goals that stretch you wide and high.

Both paths are equally beautiful and valid. Whether you find joy in a peaceful rhythm or thrive on movement, vision, and big goals that stretch you wide and high, your journey is yours to define.

The concept behind both is the same:

Your dýnami—your inner power—lives in your authentic choice.

It resides in the quiet strength of your translucent intention. It manifests in *how* you choose to live, not *what* you choose to do.

You weren't born to blend into someone else's canvas. You were made to paint your own sky. And yes, that includes brushing your teeth and answering emails—but it also brings wonder, laughter, quirky ideas, unexpected detours, and those beautiful little sparks that make life *yours*.

On everything we've explored in the previous chapters—about authenticity and genius—this is how you embody it. Not just once in a while, but every day.

Every day, a spark. Every day, a step. Every day, your life is a living, breathing work of art.

So, don't just drag yourself out of bed when you wake up tomorrow morning.

Rise like the badass explorer you are.

Grab your metaphorical compass (or your actual coffee), and say:

"Let's see what magic today has in store."

Dynamic living doesn't mean recklessness. It's not about running around chaotically with no direction. **It's about intentional movement.** Knowing that every step, even the missteps, contributes to your evolution.

The Power of Stillness in a Dynamic Life

Here's where it gets exciting:

Dynamic living isn't just about movement—it's also about mastering stillness.

In Greek, "dynamic" comes from "δínami," meaning power. That's precisely what dynamic living is—power in motion.

Many people mistake stillness for stagnation. Stillness is one of the most dynamic forces in existence.

Think of an archer before releasing an arrow. There's that moment of complete stillness before the bowstring is let go and the arrow flies precisely. That stillness fuels authentic dynamic living—not paralysis but conscious power.

You don't have to be in constant action to be dynamic. You just have to be in the flow of your own life. Consider the greatest musicians, actors, and athletes. They don't just rush through their performances. They understand the power of **pausing, holding a moment, and allowing energy to build.**

Silence on stage is often the most potent moment in acting. In music, the space between the notes creates rhythm.

Stillness is not empty—it is filled with energy, with potential.

Stories of People Who Embody Dynamic Living

Elena: The Quiet Force of Dýnami

Elena lives in a small coastal village between olive trees and the sea. She wakes up early—not out of obligation, but because she *loves* to. Her mornings begin with stillness, a cup of chamomile tea in hand, and the soft golden light of sunrise spilling across her little kitchen. The scent of basil and sea salt lingers in her home, where the windows are always cracked just enough to let in the sound of waves.

She's not building a company or chasing headline-making goals, but she is fully alive.

Every day, Elena tends to her garden with reverence. She knows the names of every plant, talks to them like old friends, and grows food with love—basil, tomatoes, figs, and mint. She takes long walks with her dog and greets her neighbors by name. She listens when people speak, not to respond, but to understand.

She teaches a handful of children in her home simple lessons about reading, numbers, and kindness. Her joy comes from watching a child's eyes light up when something clicks. No fame. No applause. Just meaning.

What makes Elena's life *dynamic* is not speed or spectacle. It's that she lives every day with choice, presence, and translucent intention. She has claimed her right—her *dynami*—to shape a peaceful, purposeful life that feels *true* to her.

Her dynamic living is a quiet rebellion against a world that insists bigger is better. Her genius lies in discovering wonder in small things. She may never grace a stage, but everyone who meets her leaves enriched—finding peace, calm, or even a spark of their own. She doesn't serve the day; the day serves her. Each night, before falling asleep, she whispers, "Thank you for adding wonder to my life today."

Malala Yousafzai: Courage in Motion

Malala Yousafzai embodies fearless action. At just 15, she was shot in the head by the Taliban for advocating girls' education in Pakistan. That moment could have silenced her, but instead, it fueled her global mission.

She recovered and spoke at the UN, demanding education rights for all children.

She co-authored "I Am Malala," a best-selling memoir that inspired millions.

She became the youngest Nobel Prize laureate, proving that resilience transforms adversity into influence.

Malala's dynamism is not just resilience; it's radiant defiance wrapped in vision.

She didn't merely survive—she amplified her voice. Her story illustrates that dynamic living isn't about avoiding fear or hardship but confronting them and using them as stepping stones to greater impact.

The Essence of Dynamic Living

Elena and Malala. Two women leading entirely different lives.

One walks barefoot through her garden; the other stands tall on the world's stage.

Yet both live dynamically. Because dynamic living isn't about the size of your platform—it's about the strength of your intention.

Dynamic living is not exclusive to the bold or loud.

Elena, in her quiet simplicity, and Malala, with her global courage, both prove the same truth:

Our choices define us.

- Take action *before* you feel fully ready.
- Turn heartbreak, resistance, or failure into the soil for new growth.
- Choose courage over comfort—whether speaking to the United Nations or being fully present with a child needing love.

Both Elena and Malala have faced fear, setbacks, and the unknown. But what makes them dynamic is their ability to move forward anyway—one step, one choice, one heartbeat at a time.

They remind us that regardless of where you are or what you do, living dynamically means being true to yourself and having the courage to show up—entirely, intentionally, and with a spark that is uniquely yours.

My Own Dynamic Living: A Life in Motion, A Heart Unbroken

For me, *dynamic living* has never been a concept—it has been a necessity—a heartbeat, a way to breathe when the air felt too heavy.

My life has been a rollercoaster of challenges.

I've balanced the tightrope of single motherhood, navigating years of empty pockets and tough decisions. I immigrated with two young adults, asking them to adapt to *my* choice—because sometimes, love means moving mountains and inviting others to climb them with you. I've spent years as a caregiver and a pleaser, often putting my own needs on hold so others could keep going.

Yet amidst all that, two things make me deeply proud:

I never gave up. And I never went to sleep bitter.

No matter how hard the day, no matter how extreme the circumstances—especially when facing the unimaginable while holding the hand of my most beloved soul, my child—I've made a choice.

Every night, I chose not to complain or drown in self-pity.

Instead, I nurtured myself—wrapped myself in a quiet smile—and whispered:

"Thank you."

Thank you for being alive.

Thank you for experiencing every flavor life offers—the bitter, the sweet, the strange.

Thank you for growing wiser through it all.

Thank you for giving me the strength to evolve into someone more whole, present, and free.

Even today, when the path remains challenging, I live dynamically—not because life is smooth, but because I continue to show up with heart. Every moment—painful or beautiful—contributes to the mosaic of my becoming.

That is my *dýnami*.

That is the quiet revolution I live each day.

Techniques to Cultivate a Dynamic Life

1. Say "Yes" More Often

Ever noticed how the most interesting things in life happen when you least expect them? That's because life doesn't always knock—it barges in, unannounced, ready to shake things up.

Like the man who agreed to teach one workshop at a local library—and discovered his passion for mentoring.

Next time an opportunity or challenge presents itself, resist the urge to say, *"I don't know... I'm not ready."* Instead, **say yes.** Trust that you will figure it out as you go. No one is ever "ready." The magic happens in the doing.

2. Say "No" More Often

Saying yes to everything is the fastest way to drain your energy and dilute your purpose.

Now, here's the flip side that most people forget:

Sometimes, dynamic living means being still. It means saying no to distractions that detract from your authenticity, peace, or priorities.

Say no to conditioning.

Say no to people-pleasing.

Say no to toxic patterns.

Say no to overcommitting just to feel "productive."

Every "no" creates space for the right "yes."

Saying no isn't harmful—it's a boundary, a declaration of clarity, and one of the most potent tools in designing your dynamic life.

3. Stay Curious Like a Child

Remember when you were a kid, and everything was fascinating? When you asked a million "why" questions and saw possibilities in every situation? That curiosity is still within you—you buried it under responsibilities, routines, and what you think is adulthood.

Dynamic living means reviving that curiosity. Ask questions. Try new things. Be more amazed than afraid.

4. Treat Challenges Like a Game

Life will throw obstacles at you—that's a guarantee. But instead of viewing them as problems, start seeing them as levels in a video game. Every challenge is an opportunity to level up.

Got rejected? Good. You just unlocked a new resilience skill.

Failed at something? Perfect. You gained wisdom you didn't have before. Feeling lost? Excellent. That means you're on the edge of something new.

Approach challenges like a quest—each one a new terrain to navigate, each failure a power-up in disguise.

5. Embrace Change Like an Old Friend

Change isn't an enemy—it's the most loyal companion you'll ever have. The sooner you make peace with it, the easier dynamic living becomes. Instead of fearing change, ask: *"What new possibilities does this bring?"*

Dynamic people don't just cope with change. They dance with it.

6. The "Freeze-the-Moment" Technique

Want to feel the energy of stillness in your body? Try this exercise:

Body Positioning:

- Sit comfortably in a chair.
- Place your buttocks firmly on the seat and your bare or socked feet flat on the floor.
- Rest your palms on your knees, facing upward.
- Join your thumb (wholeness) and index finger (individual consciousness), relaxing the other three fingers.

This gesture releases the states of dreaming, sleeping, and wakefulness, transitioning you to a fourth state—connection with wholeness.

Spinal Alignment & Energy Connection:

- Keep your spine upright, imagining an invisible thread from the stratosphere gently pulling you upward.
- Visualize this thread passing through all your chakras and extending down through your coccyx, floor, earth layers, and into the planet's core, grounding you in stability and infinite energy.

Breathing Technique:

- Take eight deep breaths, focusing on diaphragmatic movement.
- Inhale deeply for four counts, allowing the belly button to sink toward the spine.
- Exhale slowly for eight counts, expanding the diaphragm outward.
- As you breathe, visualize your spinal cord glowing white with radiant gaps between each disc.

Mental & Emotional State:

- Feel your body becoming lighter, infused with empathy and love.
- Allow your lips to form a gentle smile, reinforcing the experience of inner joy and connection.
- Remain in this meditative state for as long as possible.

Closing the Practice:

- Bring your palms together in front of your heart chakra, with your fingers straight and joined.
- This gesture expresses gratitude, closing the energy circuit within your body.
- Stay in the flow of your inner light and body's elementary energy for eight breaths.
- Open your eyes and return to the present moment. This moment of stillness isn't *nothing*. It's where your power gathers. Stillness is preparation for the next great movement.

Dynamic Living: This Is It

Dynamic living isn't about waiting for the "right moment." It's about recognizing that *now* is already full of potential. It's about saying **yes** before you feel entirely ready, following **curiosity** instead of comfort, and using challenges not as roadblocks but as fuel for growth. It's understanding that even **stillness** is part of the movement.

And no, you don't need a flawless plan.

You just need *momentum*. A spark.

One small action. And then another.

Keep Moving, Keep Growing

Remember that version of you who felt stuck? The one who hesitated, doubted, and waited for certainty? The one who let "someday" replace "today"?

That version has served its purpose—but it's no longer in charge. You're here now.

Ready. Capable. Already in motion.

Life is not a dress rehearsal.

This is it.

This moment is your canvas. Paint it with presence.

So keep moving. Keep growing. Keep becoming the person your future self will thank you for.

Now that you've embraced what it means to live dynamically, what comes next?

How do you achieve *big* things without losing your *inner* stillness? How do you stay grounded while reaching higher?

How do you create a successful life of meaning, balance, and **deep** joy?

In the next chapter, we'll explore mastering the outer world and your inner landscape so you can live with purpose, passion, and peace.

Let's go.

CHAPTER 12

The Alchemy of Peace and Power

Inner Peace, Real Power, and the Myth of "Having It All"

Recall a time when you had everything you thought you wanted—a prestigious job title, a seemingly perfect relationship, a list of hard-earned accomplishments. Yet, a nagging feeling persisted, like you were running on empty. This stark contrast between outer success and inner peace is crucial.

You looked like a shiny sports car parked in the driveway—impressive from the outside, but with no fuel in the tank. You weren't moving; you were surviving.

On the inside, something deeper was stirring.

That feeling? That's your soul waving a red flag, whispering—or maybe **screaming—Hey, you're winning the wrong game.**

Success without peace? That's burnout in disguise.

Like the executive who hit every milestone but cried quietly during layovers, unsure why nothing felt like enough.

We live in a world that glorifies the hustle. Your value is measured by how productive, busy, or impressive you appear. Exhaustion is romanticized, and resting feels like a guilty pleasure. But ask yourself honestly:

What about inner success?

What about waking up and feeling whole, even before checking your phone?

What about feeling grounded, calm, and at home in your skin—without needing applause to validate your existence?

Here's a radical idea:

Real success isn't just about conquering the outer world but about not losing yourself in the process.

Ego vs. Confidence: Know the Difference

Confidence is quiet. It knows its worth. It builds others up.

Here's where it gets interesting.

Understanding the distinction between ego and confidence can be liberating. Many people mistakenly equate **ego** with confidence, and this misunderstanding can be a significant barrier to inner peace. The relief that comes from this understanding is like a beacon of light in a dark tunnel, empowering you to navigate your journey toward inner peace.

Ego performs. It's loud, competitive, always seeking applause—yet at its core, it's terrified of not being enough.

Living from ego damages relationships.

It creates resentment in partnerships, tension in friendships, and toxicity at work. The ego doesn't know how to listen or love; it only knows how to survive, which is different from living.

The Beasts Within: What Happens When You Ignore Peace

Let's go mythological for a moment.

In ancient Greek mythology, fierce underworld goddesses called the **Erinyes** were spirits of vengeance who pursued those who violated natural and moral laws. But more than just mythical punishers, the Erinyes symbolize something deeper: the inner torment we carry when we betray truth, love, or the sacred order of life.

When you live out of alignment—ignoring the needs of others, allowing your ambition to be fueled by fear, comparison, or control—you **don't get away with** it. You may succeed on paper, but you carry the price in your chest: guilt, restlessness, anxiety, and emptiness.

You breathe with beasts inside your lungs—guilt, fear, the ache of pretending too long. These are the costs of ignoring what matters most.

And that, my friend, is its form of torture.

So don't make the mistake of envying those who seem to "have it all" but are secretly ruled by ego. They may be driven, but often they're just running from themselves.

Ambition: The Good Kind vs. The One That Breaks You

Let's talk about ambition—it's not the enemy.

Wrong ambition is fueled by ego. It wants more to *feel* like more.

"If I don't achieve this, I'm nothing."

It's competitive, draining, and ultimately unsatisfying. You hit one goal, immediately chasing the next, wondering why you're still unhappy. If you constantly compare your success to others or feel inadequate unless you achieve a certain level of success, you might be driven by the wrong ambition.

But **healthy** ambition? That's a game-changer.

It's not about being *better than* others; it's about being *better aligned with* yourself.

It's the quiet, powerful force that says:

"I want to grow so I can give. I want to learn so I can serve.

I want to build not to impress but to create something meaningful." That kind of ambition doesn't burn you out—it lights you up. It makes you **more you,** not less.

It creates success that includes rest, relationships, and joy.

Inner Peace is a Necessity

Inner peace isn't a luxury—it's your fuel. It helps you show up in the world without losing yourself.

Peace isn't passivity. It's clarity.

It's walking into a room without needing to dominate it. It's knowing your worth without having to prove it. It's being strong enough to pause, reflect, and choose presence over performance.

Now that we've gently untangled the knots around healthy ego and ambition (go you!), let's lean into something even softer:

What is inner peace—with or without them?

And what's that one tender ingredient that brings it all together like a warm cup of tea on a rainy day? Here's the sweetest secret: **It's love.**

Not the dramatic, movie-scene kind, but the quiet kind. The kind that sees you in your mess and still says, *"You're doing beautifully."*

At the core of it all—beneath confidence, clarity, authenticity, genius, dynamic

living, and peace—is one thing:

Love.

Love: The Root of Real Peace

Inner peace doesn't demand perfection. It just needs presence. It's love in motion—toward yourself, others, and the moment you're living. Love allows space for all of it: the tears, the laughter, the growing pains, the joy. Most importantly, it connects you to the part of you that was never broken to begin with.

Take a deep breath. You're already closer than you think.

Let's say it simply: Inner peace fades in the presence of judgment, shrinks in comparison, and disappears when we forget we're all connected.

And yet, we do forget. We judge. We isolate. We carry grudges like they're treasures.

But what we're missing is the most transformative, grounding, and healing force of all:

Love.

Love as a state of being. Love that lives in your breath, your choices, your compassion.

Love that says: "I'm human, you're human. Let's meet there."

Love doesn't just complete peace—it animates it. It makes stillness feel safe and motion feel meaningful.

It's what allows you to release the grip on resentment. Stop trying to be right all the time. Stop fighting yourself.

Love is the bridge between peace and power. The steady plank beneath your bare feet as you cross uncertainty.

Love Was the Answer All Along: My Journey to Balancing Peace and Purpose

Here's what I've come to know—deep in my bones: Inner peace doesn't come from escaping life. It comes from learning how to *live* it fully. Boldly. Lovingly.

For me, peace is no longer about running away to a mountaintop (though I wouldn't say no to one with good views and strong coffee). It's about balance. It's about being a grounded, compassionate leader who can make a real impact in the world—and a barefoot human who needs stillness, starlight, and the sound of animals breathing nearby. It's about being wildly intuitive—connected to something more profound—and fiercely practical, turning vision into action and soul into structure.

I used to think I had to choose: be the "spiritual one" or the "successful one." The nurturer or the warrior. The soft or the sharp. But life whispered back: *You're not here to choose. You're here to integrate.*

I see now that peace isn't the absence of ambition—it's the compass that gives ambition meaning.

I had to learn to set boundaries even when my instinct was to save the day. I had to prioritize myself—not out of selfishness but out of self-respect. I had to unlearn the idea that needing quiet meant I was weak or that my ambition was something to hide.

And the key to it all? Love. Not the poetic idea of it—but the lived experience. Loving *both* sides of myself. The dreamer and the doer. The quiet and the powerful.

When I stopped judging either part of myself and apologizing to others for being multidimensional, peace finally arrived—not as a finish line but as a presence, a rhythm, a truth.

So if you're like me—trying to lead, serve, succeed, rest, and feel—please hear this: You don't have to choose.

You just have to love the whole of who you are. That's the secret no one tells you: Love isn't just part of the answer.

Strategies for Cultivating Peace Amidst Chaos

1. The Power of Mindful Pausing

Have you ever noticed how the most successful people don't rush? They move with **calm precision**. They understand that **speed is not power—presence is.**

Like the nurse who glides calmly between beds or the CEO who listens before responding—their presence creates safety.

Take intentional pauses before responding. Breathe deeply before making decisions.

Slow down to speed up effectively.

Peace doesn't mean doing less—it means acting with **intention**.

2. Master the Art of Boundaries

A peaceful mind is a **protected** mind. You will burn out if you're always available, saying yes, and absorbing others' problems.

Learn to say **no** *without guilt.*

Create **sacred time** *for yourself daily.*

Surround yourself with people who **respect your energy.**

True peace is found not in solitude but in holding your energy no matter where you are.

3. The Observer Meditation: Becoming Your Guide

Want a powerful tool to cultivate inner peace **right now**? Try the Observer Meditation.

How to do it:

*Lie down somewhere comfortable in dim lighting and silence. Close your eyes and take **eight deep breaths**.*

*Visualize **an observer version of yourself** watching over you from above. Let the observer lead the way.*

Feel your physical form.

Observe your thoughts and gradually release them. Observe your feelings and gradually release them.

Imagine this observer stepping into your body, merging with you.

*Experience **oneness**, where there is no separation between you and your surroundings.*

Allow yourself to exist in this state of stillness.

Returning to reality, **you'll feel lighter, more transparent, and more connected to your true self.**

4. From Reaction to Response: A Loving Way to Live

Stop personalizing pain. Start witnessing it with compassion.

See every experience—even the hard ones—as a doorway, a chance to transform.

Ask:

What is this here to teach me?

How can I respond instead of react?

How can I turn this moment into something rooted in love?

With awareness, reflection, and breath—you shift. You soften. You rise.

5. Memorize: The Mantra of Love, The Map to Peace

I am Love.

Love is the space where everything makes sense.

Love just is.

Love sees my wholeness.

Love is the quiet force that dissolves time, space, and fear—and connects everything that matters.

Love transforms everything it touches.

Love is invisible, yet it fills every room I enter.
Love is nothing, yet it contains everything.

Love can't be measured.

I am Love.

6. Your Commitment Statement

"I choose to lead from peace, not pressure. I release my ego and honor my truth. I grow with love, serve with purpose, and rest without guilt. My life is mine to live—honestly, gently, and boldly."

7. The Power of Gratitude: A Gateway to Peace

One of the simplest yet most profound ways to cultivate peace is through **gratitude.**

At the end of each day, regardless of what happened, say: *Thank you. Even if the day drained you, express gratitude for the lessons.*

Even if you lost something, be thankful for the space it created.

Even if circumstances were challenging, say thank you for another day.

Gratitude shifts your perception from **lack to abundance, from fear to love.**

Personal Reflection: Where Do You Stand?

Grab a notebook and your favorite cup of tea (or coffee, no judgment), and take a few quiet minutes to reflect. Be honest. Be kind. This is about you—not perfection.

1. Ego or Confidence?

Am I chasing ego or living from essence? Do I feel the need to prove myself often?

Do I take criticism personally or defensively?

Can I celebrate someone else's success without feeling smaller? Do I listen to others without interrupting or needing to be right?

When I succeed, is it for validation or joy?

Your insight:

What's one way I can shift from ego-driven responses to confidence-rooted choices?

2. Peace or Pressure?

How often do I feel calm during the day—numb or distracted but truly at peace?

Do I constantly feel rushed, even when there's no deadline? Can I say "no" without guilt?

Do I need external achievements to feel valuable? What brings me genuine inner peace?

Your insight:

What's one small practice I can start doing daily to protect or cultivate inner peace?

3. Healthy or Harmful Ambition?

Why do I want to succeed? Is it rooted in love, growth, or fear?

Am I sacrificing my well-being to chase a goal?

Do I enjoy the process, or am I only focused on the result? Does my ambition help or harm my relationships?

What does "meaningful success" look like to me—not society, not my parents, but me?

Your insight:

How can I realign my ambition with my values and inner peace?

4. Your Erinyes Check-In

Are there "beasts" in my chest—resentments, regrets, guilt, or shame I haven't faced?

Am I carrying the emotional cost of living out of alignment with my values? Am I feeding the beasts or calming the waters?

What would my life look like if I led from peace, not guilt?

What am I doing today that my future self will thank me for—or regret?

Your insight:

What's one choice I can make this week that brings me closer to harmony with myself and others?

Remember the Inner Battles Before Achieving Balance

Success and peace **are not opposites.** They are partners. From now on, you have a different way of achieving—a way where success doesn't come at the cost of your well-being. Picture reaching your goals while remaining present, centered, and energized. Envision accomplishment without burnout, progress without stress, and fulfillment that is not just external but deeply internal.

You are working toward success that doesn't just look good—it feels good. You want a life where balance and achievement coexist, where you thrive without sacrificing your inner peace. The real victory isn't just in what you accomplish; it's in how you experience the journey.

Inner peace provides clarity and enables better decisions, leading to sustainable success.

Now that you know how to balance inner peace with outer success, what's next? It's time to go even deeper—to align your life with your deepest desires and purpose.

In the next chapter, we'll explore how to identify and pursue what truly ignites your soul. You are allowed to thrive and feel whole at the same time.

CHAPTER 13
The Fulfillment of Deepest Desires

The Joy of Indulging in Your True Desires

Desire deeply!

Close your eyes and imagine waking up one morning in the life you've always wanted. Not just a life that appears good on the outside but **feels** right—one that resonates with the deepest parts of your soul.

What does it look like? Are you working on something you love? Surrounded by uplifting people? Traveling the world? Living in a peaceful home filled with warmth and laughter? Or maybe you're finally embracing your creative side, fearlessly painting, writing, building, or performing?

Let the feeling linger a moment longer... because this is more than a fantasy—it's a glimpse into what your soul truly craves.

Now, snap back to reality—are you on the path to **that** life, or are you living a version conditioned by others? Because here's the hard truth:

Most people don't know what they truly desire. They chase what they've been told to want—money, status, approval—without pausing to ask: Is this mine, or someone else's idea of success?

Desire. That sparkly little firestarter in your brain that whispers,

"Hey... you want this. No, you need this."

It can manifest as a sudden craving for chocolate cake at 11:47 p.m., a bold vision of your future self giving TED Talks in Paris, or a specific dream of quitting your job to open a smoothie bar on a beach with a parrot named Socrates. It could be the desire for a loving relationship, a fulfilling career, or a sense of purpose in life.

Whatever the flavor, desire keeps life interesting—and occasionally a little chaotic.

But what is it?

Desire is your internal GPS, but if you haven't updated the map (aka your beliefs), you'll keep rerouting through someone else's dream.

It's the pull toward something more—more comfort, connection, knowledge, and meaning. It's the emotional GPS guiding us toward love, success, fulfillment, purpose, or the peace of feeling genuinely seen. But here's the catch: if you don't check your values and belief system first, that GPS might lead you straight into a ditch.

Sometimes it's biological—like hunger, safety, or the need to pee during a long meeting. Other times it's existential—like the desire to matter, create, or touch something sacred.

Human history is a group project powered by desire—with mixed results.

Philosophers have wrestled with this beast forever:

Plato called desire a wild horse. Buddha suggested letting go of wanting. Nietzsche said to go full throttle. Whatever the philosophy, the truth remains—desire is not the enemy. It's energy.

It fuels every painting, poem, invention, kiss, and revolution.

It's also behind most impulse purchases and questionable text messages.

The trick?

Don't suppress desire. Instead, let curiosity guide you in understanding it. Where is it coming from? What's it asking for? And most importantly, is it leading you to joy or just to Amazon Prime?

Once you stop judging desire and start listening to it, you need a way to navigate it wisely. That's where your inner GPS comes in.

Desire: Your Life's GPS (But Only If You Know How to Read the Map!)

Real fulfillment comes from the desires born at your core— the ones that light you up, make you restless if ignored, and feel alive when pursued. Anything else is borrowed, and borrowed dreams will always leave you empty.

If your life doesn't ignite your passion, you're probably living someone else's dream.

If you constantly feel restless, it means your deepest desires are knocking, and you're ignoring them.

If you're afraid to admit what you truly want, it's time to break free and own it.

The fulfillment of desire isn't about materialism or selfishness. It's about **aligning with your purpose, your soul's calling.** When you do that, you thrive, and the world benefits from the gifts you were meant to share. This is your inspiration, your motivation, your reason to pursue your true desires.

Your desires are only as good as the foundation they're built on.

Think of it this way: if your values and beliefs are unclear, shaky, or inherited from someone else (parents, society, an outdated version of yourself), then your desires are just borrowed dreams, not your true ones. Nothing is more exhausting than chasing a life that isn't yours. This is a moment for introspection, a time to contemplate your true desires and the foundation they're built on.

So, before you let your desires run wild, it's time to check your **brand values**—yes, you are a brand, whether you realize it or not. Your identity is shaped by your **values and beliefs**, which influence how you see yourself, the world, and this wild game we call life. Your brand values are the core principles that guide your decisions and actions. If you don't define them clearly, life will do it for you, likely throwing in unnecessary detours and existential confusion just for fun.

Who Are You (Really)?

Before making any significant decisions, ask yourself:

- *How do I perceive myself?*
- *What do I believe about the world and my role in it?*
- *What's my definition of self-worth (not money-wise, but in terms of purpose and fulfillment)?*
- *Am I making choices based on my true self, or just playing a role to fit in?*

Pause and write your answers. Let them surprise you.

Perception: The Invisible Script Running Your Life

Here's where it gets interesting—**perception** is how you decode, organize, and interpret everything you experience.

Your brain processes external information through memory, expectations, and the meaning you attach to things. And guess what? This all happens subconsciously.

If you're not actively redefining your value system daily, you're running on autopilot—trapped in outdated beliefs, fears, and limiting stories. The good news?

You have the power to rewrite the script!

Nothing is more accurate than the **internal map** you've created about truth. Your past, patterns, and attention shape how you see reality. Change your perception, and suddenly, what seemed impossible becomes possible.

The Big Secret: What You're Struggling to Achieve, You Already Have Within You

This will blow your mind:

Everything you're fighting for externally is already inside you.

What you've been reaching for has been waiting within, not beyond.

Self-actualization? It's about realizing you are the source of everything you've been searching for.

Like the artist who stopped chasing gallery approval and created her most beloved work from her kitchen floor.

So, let's talk **real power**—not the kind that comes from external validation, but the kind that comes from:

- Accessing your spiritual power.
- Living from your authentic identity (not the roles society has assigned to you).
- Breaking free from stress, fear, and doubt.
- Cultivating intuition and inner wisdom.
- Mastering healthy communication and truthfulness in the moment.
- Redesigning your thought-feeling-action process for success.
- Achieving meditative awareness of who you are at all times.

And let's not forget the crucial part—**observing self-sabotage.** Yes, that sneaky voice convinces you to stay small, doubt yourself, or delay your dreams. Time to kick it to the curb.

Your New Superpower: Transforming Weakness into Strength

This is the turning point—when your shadows stop being obstacles and start becoming guides. Once you begin observing your patterns, you'll realize something powerful—your greatest weaknesses can become your greatest strengths. Every fear, doubt, or emotional block is a portal to wisdom.

Quick Gut Check: Craving or Calling?

Ask yourself:

- Is this about fear or freedom? Impressing others or fulfilling me?
- Will it disappear after I get it, or will it grow with me over time?
- Is it urgent or essential? (There's a difference!)
- Does it feel like expansion or escape?

You'll know. Your body knows. Your intuition knows. Soul desires feel like home, even if they scare you a little.

Cravings feel like noise, even when they're wrapped in glitter.

Practice: The 3-Breath Desire Pause

Before you chase a desire—big or small—try this:

Breathe in and name the desire out loud. ("I want to quit my job and open a cat yoga retreat.")

Breathe out and ask: "Where is this coming from?"

Breathe again and listen to the whisper beneath the want.

Suppose it's peace, purpose, connection, or growth. It's probably worth following.

If it's panic, comparison, or proving something, maybe wait a beat.

Want to know what it looks like in the wild? Here's what happens when real people follow that whisper inside—and let it lead.

Dared to Desire: Real People, Remarkable Transformations

Whether it's the barista who became a bestselling author or Walt Disney sketching dreams in mouse ears, they're not so different. One lives next door, the other lives on your screen—but both are moved by the same inner truth: **desire**. It's not fame or fortune that sets them apart—it's the quiet courage to follow what called them. Famous or familiar, they all dared to say yes to the whisper within.

The Barista Who Became a Bestselling Author

Lydia worked at a coffee shop, quietly writing in her notebook between shifts. Despite the odds, she followed her desire to tell stories. Rejected by countless publishers, she persisted—and one day, her book became a bestseller. She never chased success. She pursued her truth.

The Mother Who Became a Community Leader

Sofia always wanted to uplift her struggling neighborhood but felt powerless. Still, she started small—organizing local events, advocating for change, and bringing people together. Her passion grew into a movement; today, she's a leader who transformed her community.

The Office Worker Who Became a World Traveler

David worked a nine-to-five job, but his heart belonged to adventure. One day, he quit, bought a one-way ticket, and started documenting his travels. His blog became a source of inspiration for thousands, proving that a life of desire-led choices is possible.

Walt Disney Who Was Sketching Dreams in Mouse Ears

Walt Disney was fired from a newspaper for "lacking creativity" and faced financial ruin multiple times. But he stayed true to his vision of creating magical stories and experiences, ultimately building one of history's most beloved entertainment empires.

Vincent van Gogh, Who Turned the Sky into a Swirling Symphony of Stars

Vincent van Gogh never painted for fame or fortune; he painted because his soul demanded it. Though unrecognized in his lifetime, his work forever changed the art world.

Nikola Tesla: Who Lit the World with an Idea

Despite financial struggles and industry opposition, Nikola Tesla pursued revolutionary ideas in energy and wireless technology. His innovations continue to shape modern life.

Frida Kahlo: Who Turned Her Wounds into Wonder

Despite lifelong pain and adversity, Frida Kahlo transformed suffering into breathtaking art that expressed her identity, heritage, and resilience. She didn't paint to sell; she painted to tell her truth.

My Beautifully Chaotic Journey of Wanting Things (and Wanting Them Again)

Following my true desires required courage—stepping away from comfort, embracing uncertainty, and defying expectations.

People told me, *"It's impossible."* They questioned my interdisciplinary approach: *"What does an actress have to do with science?"* Yet, I found allies—scientists, artists, and visionaries—people driven to uncover deeper truths. They see how the arts, physics, and behavioral sciences can illuminate new perspectives. I live in alignment with my purpose. I no longer strive to find it; **I am it**. My desires led me here, and for that, I feel profound gratitude every single day.

Your Desire Roadmap: From Craving to Clarity (and a Few Glorious Detours)

You want things. We all do.

But this isn't just about dream boards and morning affirmations. It's about choosing your life with intention—not letting it be chosen for you by your past, parents, peers, or social media algorithms.

If you're ready to follow the loop of your splendid, wild desires—and turn it into a path of actual growth—then keep reading.

If not? Go back and re-read this book. And about 20 others. Because you are not here to play small.

If your life feels off, check the roots of your dreams. Are they truly yours or inherited from someone else's expectations?

Step 1: Get Brutally Honest with Yourself

Write down what you really want. Then ask: Does this reflect my truth or my training?

Step 2: Identify What's Holding You Back

Fear of failure? Fear of judgment?

Fear of success (yes, that's real)?

Fear of success might sound like: "What if I make it and can't sustain it? What if they expect more than I can give?"

Acknowledge the blocks and dismantle them one by one. Your deepest desires won't wait forever.

Step 3: Redefine Your Belief System

Redefine your values—clearly and boldly. Without them, you'll chase what doesn't nourish you.

Redefine them. Consciously. Truthfully. Emotionally. Spiritually. Boldly.

This unlocks:

- Higher performance without burnout
- Freedom from the emotional weight you didn't even know you were carrying
- The ability to show up as you, no matter the room or role
- A deeper, juicier relationship with the present moment (yes, now counts)

Step 4: Start Small but Start Now

You don't need a grand plan. Just take one step.

Want to be an artist? Pick up a brush today.

Want to travel? Research flights.

Want to switch careers? Send that first email.

Momentum creates magic.

Step 5: Peel It Back. Meet Your Real Self.

You don't need to become someone else—remember who you were before the world told you who to be. This isn't about adding more; it's about subtracting the lies, the noise, the 'not enough,' and the ego armor.

How?

- Trust your **senses**—including that inner knowing you've been told to ignore
- Watch your **language**. Words are spells. Speak differently, live differently.
- Map your **inner world**. Know your triggers, truths, and terrain.
- Align with an **ethos** that nourishes—not punishes—your spirit.
- Understand your **ego, subconscious, and higher self**—they're not enemies; they're a team.

Step 6: Surround Yourself with Expanders

Your environment shapes you. If you're surrounded by people who settle, you pay. If you're with dreamers, risk-takers, and doers, guess what?

You'll start making things happen, too.

Step 7: Align with the Energy of Your Desire

Act as if.

If your dream self is a writer, show up every day with a notebook, a deadline, and the confidence of someone being read.

Embody the version of you that already possesses what you desire. Speak, move, and make decisions like them.

The future you is already **within you**—activate it now.

Step 8: Master the Tools That Move You Forward

- The Empathy Triangle (remember? ego-subconscious-higher self) – Understand how you relate, respond, and react.
- The Frames of your Being – Learn which **'you'** is showing up—and why.
- Align your Perception – Not just how you see things, but how you flow.
- Mind-Body-Soul Integration – You're not just a brain in a body; you are a full-spectrum masterpiece!

Step 9: Balance Desire with Ethical Living

Pursuing your desires isn't about selfishness; it's about alignment. When your desires stem from love, not ego, they serve both you and the world.

Genuine desire: "I want financial success to create, give back, and support my loved ones."

Ego-driven want: "I want financial success to prove my worth to others."

See the difference? **Follow the first.** Let go of the second.

Rewrite Your Story, Redefine Your Life

This isn't about chasing every shiny want; it's about tuning into the whispers that feel like home. It's about listening for the desires that stem from your **most profound truth**— the ones that resonate when you listen closely.

When your desires align with your highest values, they transform from wild impulses into **a roadmap**—clear, guided, and soul-approved. They indicate what you want and who you're meant to become.

So pause. Before your next big decision—or even your next small one—ask yourself:

Is this desire a reflection of my truth or a reaction to fear?

Check your inner compass. Revisit your values. Question the beliefs handed to you. Observe the lens through which you're looking.

Here's the secret: when you move from that clarity, **life meets you with magic**. Even when it's hard, you won't feel lost; you'll be **lit up** from the inside out.

So go on.

Align your desires. Rewrite your story. Redefine your life.

This isn't about becoming someone else.

It's about finally becoming you—fully, unapologetically, powerfully.

You've awakened your power. You've honored your truth.

You've dared to want more—and to want better.

At the end of your life, you won't regret the chances you took to fulfill your true desires. You'll regret not listening to your soul when it whispered to you. Trust that your desires are guiding you to your highest purpose. Choose to embody the masterpiece you are—not later, not next month, not after the next crisis, but now.

Let desire become the compass that leads you back to yourself.

CHAPTER 14

Drafting Your Masterpiece Life

Your Life as a Living Work of Art

Imagine your life as a grand work of art—one that is in constant evolution. Every moment, every decision, and every experience becomes a brushstroke, shaping a masterpiece that is uniquely yours. Some strokes are bold and intentional, driven by clarity and purpose. Others are soft and hesitant, shaped by doubt, fear, or unexpected turns. Some colors explode with the vibrancy of joy, success, and love, while others seep into the canvas with the deep, complex hues of pain, loss, and uncertainty.

The beauty of art lies not in perfection but in depth, contrast, and the interplay of light and shadow. True masterpieces emerge not from uniformity but from a willingness to embrace both the radiant and the raw, the ordered and the chaotic.

Drafting your masterpiece life means allowing yourself to imagine bigger, live more authentically, and revise as needed. It means honoring both shadows and light as essential elements of art.

Yet, here's the question: Are you actively designing this canvas, or letting others doodle on it for you?

Are you choosing the colors? Have you decided the size of your canvas? Do you even know the theme of your painting?

If you do not take charge of your masterpiece, rest assured that something or someone else will. Not your family, not your boss, not your friends, not the government, and not even your mentors should direct your strokes.

This is your art, your legacy, your life.

Go ahead—sketch, scribble, and rewrite the parts that no longer fit. This is your masterpiece, and only you can create it.

Freedom: The Original Creative Force

Freedom begins with perspective—and that's where the artist's eye transforms even pain into purpose.

To paint your masterpiece, you must first set yourself free.

Free from the shackles of doubt.

Free from the weight of past regrets.

Free from the illusion that life is happening to you rather than as you.

Everything in life—the glorious and the grotesque—has its place in the composition. Nothing occurs randomly. There is meaning in everything, even in moments that seem unbearable.

Bliss hides within the struggle, wisdom lies in pain, and strength emerges from vulnerability. The universe does not waste a single experience; each moment is a stroke of genius on your evolving canvas.

You must train your eyes to see the light in the darkness, the beauty in the ugliness, the harmony in the chaos. The world does not become beautiful simply because everything is easy; it becomes stunning because you dare to perceive it that way. Those who master life do not wait for beauty to arrive; they create it, even in the most unlikely places.

The Power of Deliberate Choices in Shaping Life

Your masterpiece life is crafted choice by choice, each a brushstroke on the canvas of your existence. You have the power to choose the colors, shapes, and themes. Your life is not a predetermined script, but a blank canvas awaiting your creative touch.

Are you choosing exciting and challenging experiences or playing it safe?

Are you surrounding yourself with people who inspire you or those who drain your energy?

Are you saying "yes" to opportunities that align with your purpose or settling for what's convenient?

Every choice is a brushstroke. The more intentional your decisions, the more vibrant and meaningful your masterpiece becomes.

Merging Creativity with Life Planning

What if you approached your life with the same passion, imagination, and creativity as an artist creating their finest work?

- Design your lifestyle like an architect. Sketch out what you want down to the details.
- Compose your relationships like a musician. Create harmony by choosing the right people to share your journey.
- Innovate your career like an inventor. Keep evolving, experimenting, and building new paths.
- Edit your thoughts like a writer. Remove limiting beliefs and rewrite your internal narrative.

The most creative people refuse to live a "paint-by-numbers" life.

Are you ready to ditch the template and create something original?

The Role of Love and Gratitude in Your Masterpiece Life

Every great artist creates from a place of love and gratitude. The same applies to life. Love and gratitude are the golden threads that weave through the fabric of your journey—when you live with love, your masterpiece radiates beauty, and when you embrace gratitude, it gains depth and meaning.

Love yourself enough to pursue what ignites your passion.

Love others deeply, knowing that human connection enriches your experience.

Be grateful for every experience—good or bad—because they all add texture to your journey.

Gratitude is like adding golden highlights to your painting. Even in the darkest corners of your journey, gratitude brings light.

It is like saying each night, "Thank you for today," "Thank you for the lessons," or "Thank you for another brushstroke on my masterpiece."

To shape with wisdom, we must understand the forces within us—enter the dance of energy.

Beneath love and gratitude lie two primal energies that quietly shape every masterpiece we create.

Root and River: Embracing and Uniting the Power of Feminine and Masculine Energies to Create Wholeness

Lastly, I want to highlight a profoundly important theme shaping every area of our lives, often without us realizing it. This theme holds more weight than ever because it influences how we relate to ourselves and others and build the world around us. It affects our choices, well-being, creativity, and future. Recognizing and understanding it isn't just helpful—it's essential. It's the key to transformation, healing, and living with greater awareness, purpose, responsibility, and connection.

That theme is timeless and persistently resurfaces—one that stirs deep within the human experience yet often remains misunderstood. One of our most intimate forces is the balance of masculine and feminine energy.

This balance—or, more often, the lack thereof—shapes our personal evolution, relationships, and the world we create. It is not about gender, roles, or external definitions imposed by history. It is about our essence—the interplay of two fundamental forces within every human being, regardless of identity, expression, or upbringing.

Feminine and Masculine Energies: What They Represent

Like the sun and the moon, these energies are not in opposition—they are complementary. Every masterpiece, whether in art, science, relationships, or personal growth, is born from the harmony of these forces. Embracing both your feminine and masculine energies is not about conforming to societal norms but about finding balance and wholeness within yourself.

Masculine Energy: The energy of focused direction, inner strength, and intentional action.

It helps you:

Organize your vision.

Create structure around your ideas and stay grounded as you move forward.

When used with awareness, it becomes a powerful ally that prevents you from repeating patterns of chaos, procrastination, or emotional overwhelm. It gives you the courage to build without fear.

Feminine Energy: The source of imagination, emotional truth, and soulful insight.

It invites you:

To listen deeply.

To feel fully.

To create meaning.

It's where your most profound ideas are born. When you honor it, you heal the wounds of the past—not by ignoring them but by transforming them into beauty and wisdom through your work. This allows your masterpiece to breathe with life and authenticity.

For instance, when launching a new project, you may rely on masculine focus to structure deadlines while using feminine intuition to guide the creative vision.

It's key to creating a masterpiece and a life that feels powerful and purposeful.

Once you understand what each energy offers, you can begin to apply them intentionally, moment by moment.

The Art of Integration: Becoming Whole

Cultivate masculine energy when you need focus, direction, and execution. Set goals, make decisions, take action, and build resilience.

Embrace feminine energy when you need inspiration, connection, and flow. Listen to your intuition, surrender to life's rhythm, create without constraints, and nurture yourself and others.

Act with discipline, plan with logic, and lead with heart. This is the dance of wholeness.

This sacred dance of existence, when balanced, brings clarity, ease, and fulfillment. It allows us to become not just successful but whole.

If enough individuals embody this harmony within themselves, the world might reflect that balance, too.

Conscious Creation: The Only Alternative to Fate

Carl Jung once said, *"Until you make the unconscious conscious, it will direct your life, and you will call it fate."*

It's a call to bravery: face what lives in the shadows, or risk living by someone else's script.

Most people drift through life believing they are victims of circumstance. They react instead of creating, accept rather than shape, and tell themselves that life is happening to them rather than recognizing the profound truth: life is responding to them.

But when you slow down enough to listen, stop numbing yourself with distractions, and face the quiet truth beneath the surface, you will see it clearly:

The masterpiece was always in your hands.

Yes, discomfort will arise. Fear will whisper its doubts. The past will try to pull you back.

You hold the palette. The canvas waits for your next bold stroke.

Do not let fate paint your life for you. Take control. Choose the colors. Shape your masterpiece with full awareness, deep intention, and the raw, unfiltered essence of who you are.

Ultimately, life is not about waiting for the perfect moment to create—it is about recognizing that every moment is the most valuable stroke you will ever place on your canvas.

Live boldly. Create fearlessly. And make it a masterpiece.

Let your life not just be seen—but felt, remembered, and wholly lived.

CHAPTER 15

Masterpiece or Monsterpiece

Your Calling

Your Final Choice

Here we are at the final chapter. You made it.

Now, I have one simple, slightly uncomfortable, utterly liberating question for you:

Which tribe will you join—The Masterpiece or The Monsterpiece?

Too dramatic? Perhaps. But sometimes drama is the only thing louder than denial.

This drama is precisely what you need—the kind that jolts you awake from the sleepwalking scroll of society and prompts you to choose. With presence. With clarity. With the wild heartbeat of yours that still believes something greater is possible.

Here's the truth: we are living in The Reality Gap.

The Reality Gap is the space between what's happening and what we believe is happening.

One Planet, Infinite Realities

You and I share the same Earth, breathe the same air, and read the same headlines. Yet, we may inhabit entirely different mental worlds. You see a problem; someone else sees a conspiracy. You perceive progress; someone else senses collapse. You wish to heal the world; someone else debates whether the world is even sick.

It's not just disagreement anymore. It's a division at the *level of reality construction*.

Why? Because, as neuroscience reminds us, we don't see the world as it is—we see it as we are—shaped by our past, fears, programming, and beliefs—all dressed up as "truth."

So when your cousin argues with you over politics, it's not a clash of facts—it's a clash of realities. You're not disagreeing. You're living in separate universes.

This is why traditional solutions keep failing. You can't heal a split reality with a PowerPoint presentation and a motivational quote. You can't logic your way into someone else's lived perception.

They're not just playing a different game—they're on a different board.

The Tribe of Masterpieces vs. The Tribe of Monsterpieces

Here's where it gets real. Every day, you cast your vote for one of two tribes:

- **The Tribe of the Masterpiece**: people who understand that their perception creates reality. They seek to *integrate*, not to dominate. They choose curiosity over control, expansion over ego, and wholeness over winning.
- **The Tribe of the Monsterpiece**: people ruled by fear, blame, shame, and inherited programming, who unconsciously become chaos creators. They pitch, they argue, they control, and they collapse. And worst of all, they believe it's noble. They don't mean harm, but fear has taught them to fight, to shrink, to protect rather than evolve.

Which one are you becoming?

Before you say "Masterpiece, of course!"—pause. Reflect on your daily thoughts, reactions, scrolling habits, self-talk, and how you treat people who disagree with you. Are your actions *evolving you* or *excusing you*?

It's not what you say that determines your tribe. It's what you practice.

The Truth About the Monsterpiece

Let's not demonize the Monsterpiece. Most of us carry a bit of it within. That part of you throws an emotional tantrum when someone questions your worldview, that old programmed pattern whispering, *"If they don't agree with me, they're dangerous."* That impulse to be right instead of kind.

We all have our monsters.

But you get to decide whether you let yours write your story—or merely act as comic relief.

Why Choose The Masterpiece

The Masterpiece version of you is not perfect. It's not polished. It doesn't wear spiritual makeup or recite borrowed affirmations.

It's raw. Grounded. Playful. Brave. Curious.

It's the version of you that studies the self without judgment. The one who listens to the heart not for pain, but for power. The one who transforms trauma into compost, not concrete.

The Masterpiece is YOU—rewritten.

How do you rewrite yourself?

Simple. Study.

Study the world. Study the self. Study others without trying to fix them.

This is the sacred practice of our Supraconscious path. Not to *know* everything, but to *notice* everything without ego. Understand that reality is not something you inhabit—it's something you *build* from the inside out.

And then choose. Again and again.

And Finally, the Last (and Best) Truth

The world is not broken because of evil people.

It's fractured because too many are trapped in old perceptions.

But you—yes, *you*—are waking up, and with this awakening comes the potential for growth and change. This is the messy, glorious, history-making part.

So don't just change your mind.

Change the reality your mind inhabits. Don't just be good.

Be whole.

Don't wait for the future. Create the masterpiece.

It's not about making more pitches; it's about being present. The world needs your presence, your engagement, your active participation.

So the only question left is: Which one are you becoming?

Your story is unwritten. The pen is warm in your hand.

Start right now.

My Masterpeace: The ReBirth

Inspired Help for the Journey Ahead: A Blank Canvas

This is the moment.

The moment where everything you have read, felt, and questioned so far dissolves into one simple truth:

Your life is your masterpiece.

It's not mine, not your parents', not society's, not the one shaped by expectations or the voices of the past.

Yours.

Now, I step back.

No prescriptions. Just sacred questions—gentle sparks to ignite what's already inside you.

Just space—sacred, untouched space—for you to create, where your imagination is the only limit.

Where Do You Begin?

There are no rules.

How would you begin if you had the power to rewrite your life from scratch?

Would you start with a single word? A vision? A declaration? A question?

Write it. Draw it.

Let it take shape in whatever way feels most authentic to you. Take your time.

Write freely.

_____

_____

_____

_____

_____

_____

_____

_____

_____

_____

_____

_____

_____

_____

Who Are You—Without the Roles?

Strip away the labels. The roles. The expectations.

Who would you be if no one watched, judged, or expected anything from you?

Who is the person beneath everything you were told to be?

Describe yourself in your most valid form:

_____

_____

_____

_____

_____

_____

_____

_____

_____

_____

_____

_____

_____

What Do You Love?

Not what you have been told to love. Not what the world values.

Not what seems practical or impressive.

What truly moves you?
What makes your heart race?
What fills you with a quiet sense of belonging?

Make a list of everything you love—no matter how big or small:

_____

_____

_____

_____

_____

_____

_____

_____

_____

_____

_____

_____

_____

_____

_____

_____

_____

_____

_____

_____

_____

_____

_____

_____

_____

_____

_____

_____

_____

_____

_____

_____

_____

_____

Your Dream Life Without Limits

What would your life look like without fear, doubt, or restrictions?

What scents fill your kitchen? What song drifts through your morning?

How does freedom taste?

What would your days feel like? What kind of work would you do?

What kind of people would surround you?

How would you express yourself?

Describe your dream life in vivid detail:

_____

_____

_____

_____

_____

_____

_____

_____

_____

_____

Your Greatest Gifts

We all have something unique to offer the world, and your uniqueness is what makes you special.

What comes naturally to you?
What makes you feel alive when you do it?
What do people often thank you for?

Identify your unique gifts and strengths:

_____

_____

_____

_____

_____

_____

_____

_____

_____

_____

_____

_____

Your Truth—In One Sentence

If your whole soul whispered just one sentence—what would it say?

Write your personal truth statement:

_____

_____

_____

_____

_____

_____

_____

_____

_____

_____

_____

_____

_____

_____

_____

_____

The Patterns You're Ready to Break

We all carry patterns, beliefs, and habits that no longer serve us.

Which ones are you ready to release?
What thoughts or behaviors hold you back? What fears or doubts keep you small?
What old stories no longer belong in your life?

Take a deep breath. Then write down what you're ready to release:

_____

_____

_____

_____

_____

_____

_____

_____

_____

_____

_____

Your Next Step

Every life is written one heartbeat at a time.

What is one step—small or big—you can take today to move closer to your truth?

It doesn't have to be perfect. Just **one step.**

Write your next action step:

_____

_____

_____

_____

_____

_____

_____

_____

_____

_____

_____

_____

_____

_____

My MASTERPEACE in progress

This is not the final page.

This is not the last word, the full stop, or the grand finale. This is your sacred beginning.

You are not finished.

You are the living brushstroke of a more fabulous Artist, a divine symphony still being composed,

A story bursting with chapters yet to be written. So get a notebook—or many.

Let your hands become instruments of truth.

And if writing isn't your thing, then begin in the silence of your mind.

Start crafting your life with the thoughts you choose. The love you give, the dreams you dare to believe.

You are both the author and the awe-inspiring story.

You are the miracle in motion. Own it.

Honor it.

Live it—with unshakable faith, with fearless love,

With the knowing that the best is still being born through you. Enjoy your life.

Share your light. Shine your love. Always,

Maria

Online Sources

Chapter 1

Pendulum Dowsing Unlocking Deep Life Mysteries. https://plusvalueindia.com/unlocking-the-mysteries-of-pendulum-dowsing/

Chapter 2

Best Brain Gym in Jaipur: Unlock Your Mind's Potential. https://www.pragyapersonalitydevelopment.com/courses/neurobics-best-brain-gym-best-brain-gym

Chapter 3

Joel Jones – Charlottesville Podcasting Network. https://www.cvillepodcast.com/tag/joel-jones/

Chapter 4

BORN A CRIME BY TREVOR NOAH – Book lovers. https://bookloversonline.wordpress.com/2020/03/01/born-a-crime-by-trevor-noah/

Chapter 6

Transforming Your Mindset with R.E.B.T.: A Guide to Rational Emotive Behavior Therapy – Psylancer. https://psylancer.com/psychotherapeutic-modalities/

transforming-your-mindset-with-r-e-b-t-a-guide-to-rational-emotive-behavior-therapy/

Chapter 8

How to Get Better at Asking for Help at Work - Beyond leadership. https://beyondleadership.si/tip-of-the-week/how-to-get-better- at-asking-for-help-at-work/

Chapter 9

Man Loses Wife in Paris Attacks, Writes Letter to Terrorists. https://sofrep.com/news/man-loses-wife-in-paris-attacks-writes-powerful-open-letter-terrorists/

How to Get Better at Asking for Help at Work - Beyond leadership. https://beyondleadership.si/tip-of-the-week/how-to-get-better- at-asking-for-help-at-work/

Chapter X

What Were the Causes of Apartheid? https://www.reference.com/world-view/were-causes-apartheid-5fd789838e75e473

Note from the Author

Thank You for Reading Be a Masterpeace not a Monsterpeace part of the soul-awakening "Who Are You?" series by Maria Olon Tsaroucha.

If this journey moved you, awakened something within you, or left you longing for more—

There is so much more waiting.

Embark on transformative journeys and discover profound wisdom within Maria Olon Tsaroucha's works.

For Individuals, Organizations, or Visionary Teams

If you or your company seeks more profound impact, awareness, or inner mastery, consider the following immersive opportunities at www.supraconscious.co

The Supraconscious You Online Programs, Retreats, and masterclasses that expand consciousness and transform the way you live, lead, and create.

Couple & Family Courses Transformational experiences for couples and families ready to break generational patterns, deepen emotional connection, and awaken a new way of loving—together.

Custom Programs for Organizations Workshops and trainings designed to elevate emotional intelligence, creative leadership, and collective awareness.

Private Mentorship & One-to-One Immersions

For a rare opportunity to work directly with Maria Olon Tsaroucha in a personalized, intensive experience tailored to unlock your genius and align your inner and outer life send an email to info@supraconscious.co.

Your next chapter is already unfolding.

About the Author

Maria Olon Tsaroucha is a visionary thought leader, internationally acclaimed artist, educator, and author of the award-winning Amazon bestseller Supraconscious: The Genius Within You.

As the founder of the Supraconscious You platform, she has spent over two decades pioneering a humanistic, artistic, and scientific approach to consciousness, identity, and personal evolution.

Maria's work is a unique blend of ancient ethics, modern neuroscience, quantum physics, and the art of method acting. This distinctive approach allows her to delve into the profound question of 'Who Am I and How I Live as my Highest Self.'

From global stages to humanitarian missions and transformative workshops across continents, Maria's work has resonated with a diverse range of people. She is known for igniting profound shifts in scientists, artists, educators, visionaries, and seekers alike.

At the remarkable age of thirteen, Maria penned her first book, a feat that earned her the title of the youngest Greek author ever.

"Your life is not your résumé. It is your revelation."

— Maria Olon Tsaroucha

More Books by Maria Olon Tsaroucha

Embark on transformative journeys through consciousness, art, and human evolution with the visionary works of Maria Olon Tsaroucha—where science meets spirit, and the stage of life becomes a path to awakening.

SUPRACONSCIOUS: The Genius Within You

The foundational textbook of a quantum science of acting and living—where mindfulness, physics, and method merge into a new system for awakening the Higher Self.

Translucent Vacant Head

A poetic excavation of silence and memory that exposes the invisible inheritance of family wounds and transforms them into luminous truth.

Supra Guardians: The Victorious Journey of Self-Knowledge, Love, and Transformation Against the Seven Sins

A mythic odyssey of light and courage that invites young and timeless souls to remember their divine humanity and become guardians of a new world.

Not Mars. Not Venus. Just Us.

A groundbreaking revelation that ends the myth of gendered worlds, showing that men and women are not opposites but mirrors seeking authentic human connection.

Visit amazon.com/author/mariaolon
and books.by/mariaolontsaroucha